Long-Term Stage, Stage-Residual, and Width Data for Streams in the Piedmont Physiographic Region, Georgia

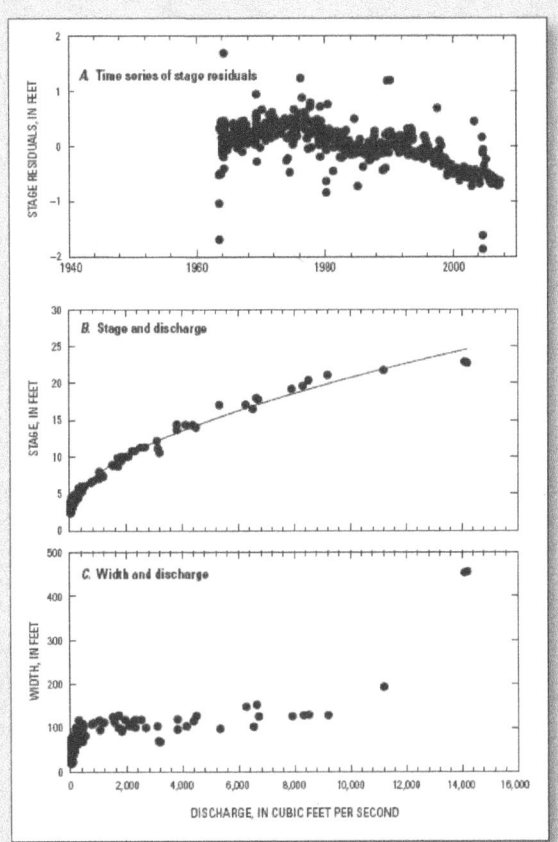

Open-File Report 2009–1205

U.S. Department of the Interior
U.S. Geological Survey

Long-Term Stage, Stage-Residual, and Width Data for Streams in the Piedmont Physiographic Region, Georgia

By Jeffrey W. Riley and Robert B. Jacobson

Open-File Report 2009–1205

U.S. Department of the Interior
U.S. Geological Survey

U.S. Department of the Interior
KEN SALAZAR, Secretary

U.S. Geological Survey
Suzette M. Kimball, Acting Director

U.S. Geological Survey, Reston, Virginia: 2009

For more information on the USGS—the Federal source for science about the Earth, its natural and living resources, natural hazards, and the environment, visit *http://www.usgs.gov* or call 1-888-ASK-USGS

For an overview of USGS information products, including maps, imagery, and publications, visit *http://www.usgs.gov/pubprod*

To order this and other USGS information products, visit *http://store.usgs.gov*

Suggested citation:
Riley, J.W., and Jacobson, R.B., 2009, Long-term stage, stage-residual, and width data for streams in the Piedmont physiographic region, Georgia: U.S. Geological Survey Open-File Report 2009–1205, 46 p.

Contents

Figures

Table

Conversion Factors and Datums

Multiply	By	To obtain
Length		
foot (ft)	0.3048	meter (m)
Area		
square mile (m²)	2.590	square kilometer (km²)
Flow rate		
cubic foot per second (ft³/s)	0.02832	cubic meter per second (m³/s)

Horizontal coordinate information is referenced to the North American Datum of 1983 (NAD 83) and the North American Datum of 1927 (NAD 27).

Long-Term Stage, Stage-Residual, and Width Data for Streams in the Piedmont Physiographic Region, Georgia

By Jeffrey W. Riley and Robert B. Jacobson

Abstract

This report presents the data used to assess geomorphic adjustment of streams over time and to changing land-use conditions. Thirty-seven U.S. Geological Survey streamgages were selected within the Piedmont physiographic region of Georgia. Width, depth, stage, and discharge data from these streams were analyzed to assess channel stability and determine if systematic adjustments of channel morphology could be related to time or land use and land cover. Residual analyses of stage-discharge data were used to infer channel stability, which could then be used as an indicator of habitat stability. Streamgages, representing a gradient of urbanization, were selected to test hypotheses regarding stream stability and adjustment to urban conditions. Results indicate that 14 sites exhibited long-term channel stability, 11 were degrading, 6 were aggrading, and 6 showed variability in response over the study period.

Introduction

Geomorphic adjustments to stream channels can affect the type, distribution, and quality of in-stream habitat across all scales. The method used in this study, however, is only used to infer reach scale processes that are based on channel adjustments at streamgage locations. Channel adjustments and subsequent habitat degradation are an essential component when evaluating the effects of streamflow on lotic ecosystems. Channel adjustments and the effects of habitat alteration could influence how altered streamflows will affect aquatic biota. Adjustments may result from various natural disturbances such as floods and landslides or from anthropogenic sources like stream impoundment and watershed development, which often alter runoff characteristics. In this study, natural processes were of less concern than anthropogenic stressors, as many of the gage locations are in urbanized areas and a few downstream from impoundments.

This study was conducted in support of the U.S. Geological Survey Flint River Science Thrust project, "Water Availability for Ecological Needs," which was designed to improve understanding of the relations between streamflow and ecological health (Hughes and others, 2007). The project was initiated in 2007 and includes an interdisciplinary team of geologists, geographers, hydrologists, and ecologists. The overall goal of the project is to develop predictive tools for understanding how alterations in streamflow can affect aquatic communities. As part of this effort, stream-channel morphology data were compiled and analyzed within the upper Flint River basin (UFRB) and nearby watersheds.

Water resource managers could benefit greatly from models that can be used to predict biological conditions in response to altered streamflows resulting from climatic variability or watershed development and water use. The Flint River Science Thrust project is designed to address this need by using existing datasets to develop models relating geology, geomorphology, hydrology, and land use and land cover to biological management objectives in the UFRB. Proper model calibration requires the determination of stream channel stability. If channels are in a phase of adjustment, and if instability and ongoing adjustments are large enough, they might mask or exacerbate hydrologic effects. For example, if streambeds are degrading or channel widths are increasing, water may be distributed differently across the channel. During drought periods, the effect of channel adjustments and associated water distribution may increase stress to aquatic organisms.

Channel morphology information from streamgages also can be used as an indicator for habitat conditions. By analyzing cross-sectional data from discharge measurements for long-term streamgages, overall trends of bed aggradation, degradation, or stability can be determined (James, 1991; Jacobson, 1995; Juracek and Fitzpatrick, 2009). Resultant channel behavior also can be used to infer stability and persistence of habitat conditions.

Changes in channel morphology can have a pronounced effect on available habitat in alluvial streams. For example, if a stream increases in width, less habitat volume (that is, less water depth) is available for fish and other aquatic organisms during times of low water. A decrease in depth can result in increased predation and competition, thermal stress, and diminished water quality. For these reasons, channel stability is an important consideration when establishing in-stream flow requirements or flow recommendations. Channels respond to changes in discharge and(or) sediment supply (Knighton, 1998). If sediment load is increased without an increase in discharge, the channel bed likely will aggrade. As a result, the channel will no longer be able to convey the same amount of water, and the channel will readjust in one of two ways: degrading the bed once the sediment supply is returned to pre-disturbance levels or cutting laterally, which causes the channel to widen in order to convey the amount of water delivered from upstream (Richard and others, 2005; Simon and Rinaldi, 2006). A common scenario in urbanizing drainage basins is an initial pulsed increase in sediment supply followed by a period of persistent increased runoff (Wolman, 1967), a situation that is likely to accelerate channel widening or incision.

Acknowledgments

The authors are grateful for assistance from Gary Buell, U.S. Geological Survey (USGS) Georgia Water Science Center, in obtaining data.

Purpose and Scope

The purpose of this report is to document the data used for channel stability analysis, the methods used in the analysis, and general results relating to relative channel instability in the Piedmont region of Georgia. The datasets include streamgage measurements that begin as early as 1940 and extend to 2006 and drainage areas that vary from 31 to 2,950 square miles (mi^2). Detailed analysis of relations between land use and channel instability is beyond the scope of this report.

This report presents analyses of data for the 37 streamgages studied as part of the Flint River Science Thrust project in the Georgia Piedmont (fig. 1; table 1). The streamgage locations represent varying degrees of impervious cover and flow regulation. Data from discharge measurements were obtained to analyze how the stage-discharge relation changed over time. Plots of width and discharge were generated to identify approximate bankfull stage. Graphs in figures 2–38 were produced and are included in the report:

1. Stage-discharge relation and a best-fit statistical model of the relation for the entire corrected record.

2. Time series of residuals from the modeled relation.

3. The relation between width and discharge.

Methods

Streamgages were selected for data collection to represent the longest-term records available in the Piedmont physiographic region of Georgia. Initially, streamgages in the UFRB with at least 20 years of record were chosen for analysis (table 1). This criterion limited the number of sites to only five; thus, additional gages in the Georgia Piedmont

were selected to allow a more general assessment of piedmont streams and look for patterns of adjustment or stability. Sites also were selected with varying degrees of urbanization to develop an urban to rural gradient and analyze for relations between urbanization and channel morphology. This approach uses a method known as location for time substitution (LTS) in which different streams in different stages of erosional processes can be used to represent a single stream over time (Schumm, 1991).

Discharge measurement field data were obtained from the USGS National Water Information System (NWIS) database and from paper files located at the USGS Georgia Water Science Center in Atlanta, Georgia, for selected streamgages (table 1). Station description files were obtained from the Station Information Management System (SIMS) to check for continuity in the record. Because of bridge construction or altered channel conditions at some locations, gages were moved up or downstream, and data were adjusted to correct for the relocation of the gages.

Initially, other aspects of channel form that co-vary with discharge were to be analyzed, such as width, depth, and velocity. However, the combination of wading and nonwading discharge measurements complicated this analysis. For example, wading measurements typically are made at locations that are best suited for making an accurate measurement at a given discharge; hence the actual location of the measurement may change with flow conditions, resulting in different cross sections being measured, producing different widths and average depths and velocities for a wading site. Depth, width, and velocity can be analyzed for wading measurements if discharge field notes are obtained and a sufficient number of measurements are made at specific cross sections (Jacobson, 1995). Bridge measurements are consistently made at the same location, assuming the bridge has not been rebuilt or substantially altered. If there are a sufficient number of bridge measurements, the data can be analyzed separately for changes in other channel parameters, since the same channel cross section was measured. Geomorphic analysis at bridge sites, however, can be confounded by bridge piers and abutments that limit geomorphic adjustments.

Data were corrected for a consistent gage datum as part of regular gaging operations, so it was not necessary to make datum corrections for this report. In the event that datums are changed or streamgages moved a short distance up or downstream and only the stage-discharge data are to be used, datum corrections can be applied to render all data functional. The procedure is outlined in Smelser and Schmidt (1998).

Streamgaging measurements are often the only source of long-term channel cross-sectional data available for stream channels (Juracek and Fitzpatrick, 2009). These data include measurements of width, average depth, discharge, average velocity, and stage at the time of the measurement. From these data, relations can be constructed with parameters that co-vary with discharge. This is accomplished by regressing stage against discharge similar to a rating curve, only the predictor variable (independent) is switched. For example, rather than

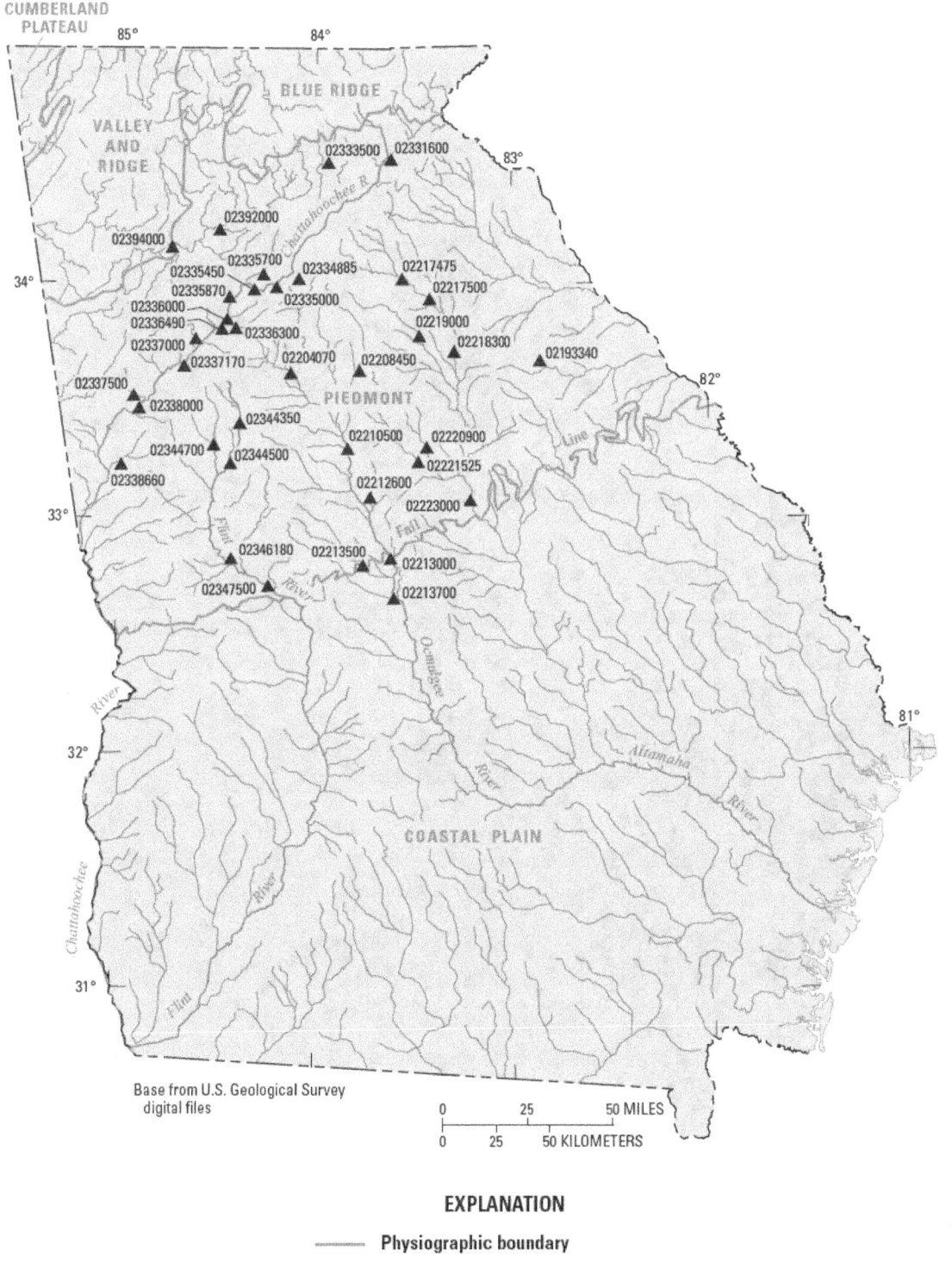

Figure 1.   Location of streamgages used for geomorphic analysis.

Table 1. Charcteristics of streamgage locations used for geomorphic analysis and corresponding figure numbers.

Station number	Station name	Response	Statistical model[a]	R^2	Mean percent impermeable	Drainage area, square miles (mi²)	Record length (years)	Figure number
02193340	Kettle Creek near Washington, GA	Degrading	Exponential, 3 parameter	0.96	0.00	34	22	9
02204070	South River at Klondike Road, near Lithonia, GA	Stable	Double exponential, 5 parameter	1.00	26.82	185	25	19
02208450	Alcovy River above Covington, GA	Degrading	Double exponential, 5 parameter	0.95	4.98	181	36	10
02210500	Ocmulgee River near Jackson, GA	Stable	Double exponential, 5 parameter	0.99	10.79	1,432	32	30
02212600	Falling Creek near Juliette, GA	Aggrading	Power, 3 parameter	0.99	0.00	72	45	15
02213000	Ocmulgee River at Macon, GA	Aggrading	Exponential, 3 parameter	0.96	7.93	2,248	57	13
02213500	Tobesofkee Creek near Macon, GA	Stable-degrading	Power, 3 parameter	0.98	1.64	185	71	38
02213700	Ocmulgee River near Warner Robins, GA	Stable	Double exponential, 5 parameter	0.99	1.64	185	37	31
02217475	Middle Oconee River near Arcade, GA	Degrading	Power, 3 parameter	0.99	4.15	332	21	8
02217500	Middle Oconee River near Athens, GA	Wavy	Power, 3 parameter	0.98	4.98	393	67	35
02218300	Oconee River near Penfield, GA	Aggrading	Power, 3 parameter	0.98	4.60	942	30	17
02219000	Apalachee River near Bostwick, GA	Stable	Double exponential, 5 parameter	0.99	3.35	176	31	22
02220900	Little River near Eatonton, GA	Degrading	Power, 3 parameter	0.98	1.02	266	21	3
02221525	Murder Creek below Eatonton, GA	Stable	Power, 3 parameter	0.96	0.34	190	31	27
02223000	Oconee River at Milledgeville, GA	Degrading	Power, 3 parameter	0.95	2.15	2,950	42	12
02331600	Chattahoochee River near Cornelia, GA	Stable	Power, 2 parameter	0.99	1.75	318	31	28
02333500	Chestatee River near Dahlonega, GA	Degraded-stabilized	Power, 3 parameter	0.93	1.20	150	68	36
02334885	Suwanee Creek at Suwanee, GA	Degrading	Double exponential, 5 parameter	0.97	12.40	46	24	2
02335000	Chattahoochee River near Norcross, GA	Stable	Power, 3 parameter	0.99	4.35	1,171	54	24
02335450	Chattahoochee River above Roswell, GA	Stable	Power, 3 Parameter	0.98	5.12	1,219	32	29
02335700	Big Creek near Alpharetta, GA	Wavy	Double exponential, 4 parameter	0.95	10.36	73	41	33
02335870	Sope Creek near Marietta, GA	Degrading	Double exponential, 5 parameter	0.98	27.06	31	24	5
02336000	Chattahoochee River at Atlanta, GA	Aggraded-stabilized	Double exponential, 4 arameter	0.97	7.69	1,451	71	37
02336300	Peachtree Creek at Atlanta, GA	Degrading	Power, 3 parameter	0.98	41.46	86	45	4

Table 1. Charcteristics of streamgage locations used for geomorphic analysis and corresponding figure numbers. —Continued

Station number	Station name	Response	Statistical model[a]	R²	Mean percent impermeable	Drainage area, square miles (mi²)	Record length (years)	Figure number
02336490	Chattahoochee Rivera at GA 280, near Atlanta, GA	Stable	Power, 3 parameter	0.99	10.42	1,591	32	26
02337000	Sweetwater Creek near Austell, GA	Aggrading	Double exponential, 5 parameter	0.99	11.64	238	71	14
02337170	Chattahoochee River near Fairburn, GA	Degrading	Power, 3 parameter	0.99	11.75	2,055	43	11
02337500	Snake Creek near Whitesburg, GA	Stable	Power, 3 parameter	0.98	2.36	35	54	20
02338000	Chattahoochee River near Whitesburg, GA	Stable	Power, 3 parameter	1.00	10.60	24,12	42	25
02338660	New River at GA 100, near Corinth, GA	Aggrading	Double exponential, 5 parameter	0.99	2.52	125	30	16
02344350	Flint River near Lovejoy, GA	Degrading	Power, 3 parameter	0.99	22.91	128	22	7
02344500	Flint River near Griffin, GA	Stable/ slightly wavy	Double exponential, 5 parameter	0.97	14.15	268	70	34
02344700	Line Creek near Senoia, GA	Degrading	Double exponential, 5 parameter	0.99	7.96	101	43	6
02346180	Flint River near Thomaston, GA.	Stable	Power, 3 parameter	1.00	5.00	1,219	28	21
02347500	Flint River at U.S. 19, near Casonville, GA	Stable	Power, 3 parameter	0.99	3.73	1,850	70	32
02392000	Etowah River at Canton, GA	Aggraded- large variance	Power, 3 parameter	0.96	1.89	614	67	18
02394000	Etowah River at Allatoona Dam, above Cartersville,GA	Stable	Double exponential, 4 parameter	0.98	4.72	1,118	69	23

[a] Model fit to stage and discharge.

using stage to predict discharge, discharge would be used to predict stage. For these analyses, curves were fit to the entire corrected record. Systematic fitting is required to find the best regression model; generally a power function or double exponential worked the best for most locations (table 1). From this regression, residual values can be obtained by subtracting predicted values from measured values. These residual values are then plotted against time to evaluate trends independent of discharge (James, 1991). Streambed changes are illustrated by the deviation of the residual from zero. If the stage-discharge relation has not changed, the trend of the residuals should be a relatively horizontal line with equal scatter above and below. If there is aggradation, the trend will be positive and negative if degrading. Because changes in the relation of stage to discharge can vary because of changes in flow velocity or channel width, it is necessary to evaluate these possibilities simultaneously.

Results

Stage-discharge data, stage-residual time series data, and width-discharge data for the 37 streamgages analyzed for this study are presented in figures 2–38. Analysis of stage-residual data indicates that streams in the Georgia Piedmont have been dynamic over the period of record. Taken as a whole, however, there were no clear, systematic trends in changes in channel morphology with land cover or drainage area. Streambed responses varied with no clearly identifiable cause for the specific type of response.

Eleven of the 37 gages analyzed showed distinct trends of degradation, as inferred from declining water-surface elevations. The magnitude of the degradation was variable as was the general form of response. Some gages exhibited a linear trend of degradation (figs. 2–3), whereas others had a somewhat wavy response or breaks in the slope of the trend. For example, Peachtree Creek at Atlanta, GA (fig. 4), Sope Creek near Marietta, GA (fig. 5), and Line Creek near Senoia, GA (fig. 6), all show a response in which the streambed degrades for a period of time, then levels off and then begins to degrade again. Figures 7–10 represent degrading sites with short periods of record where trends other than general degradation were difficult to determine. The sites with the greatest drainage area that experienced degradation were the Chattahoochee River near Fairburn, GA (fig. 11), which is in the vicinity of a sand-pumping operation, and Oconee River near Milledgeville, GA (fig. 12), which is heavily flow regulated by an upstream reservoir.

Six of the 37 sites had a trend of overall aggradation as inferred from increasing water-surface elevations. For this study, all of the aggrading trends were generally of lower mag-nitude than the degrading trends. Ocmulgee River at Macon, GA (fig. 13), was an exception to this trend as it aggraded approximately 3 feet (ft) from the beginning of the record until the mid 1990s and then started a degradation trend. Of the other sites that aggraded, Sweetwater Creek near Austell, GA (fig. 14), had a near-linear trend with the exception of a large

increase in water-surface elevation and subsequent decrease about 1965. As with degradation, some of the aggrading sites exhibited a slight wavy pattern while aggrading (figs. 15–16), whereas only one had a pronounced wavy pattern (fig. 17). The Etowah River at Canton, GA (fig. 18), aggraded steadily until about 1980; thereafter, variance increased and any discernable trend disappeared.

Fourteen of the gage locations had relatively stable ratings over the course of the record. Some of these exhibited substantial stability (figs. 19–22), lacking the scatter associated with many of the residual plots. The Etowah River below Allatoona Dam (fig. 23) exhibited similar stability, only with greater scatter of the data. The other pattern observed was general stability about a mean, but with greater variability in the residuals (figs. 24–27). Plots that demonstrated slight adjustment over the period of record were also included in this group (figs. 28–32).

Considering all of the sites examined, only one displayed a distinct wavy pattern, possibly indicative of waves of sediment passing the gage (fig. 33). Many sites had low amplitude waves; however, Big Creek near Alpharetta, GA, showed a systematic trend, with degradation occurring for about 15 years, followed by a rapid aggradation period, and then about 15 years of relative stability. The period of stability was subsequently followed by additional degradation, although to a lesser degree than the earlier episode. Most recently, Big Creek near Alpharetta, GA, began aggrading again. Two other sites are included in this category (figs. 34–35); however, their wavy patterns appear more random and are not as well defined.

A few of the gages had variable responses that made them difficult to put in a single response category. For example, at the beginning of the record, residual values at the Chestatee River near Dahlonega, GA (fig. 36), were about 2 ft above what would have been expected from the rating relation. Then the channel appears to degrade approximately 2 ft from 1940 to 1960; thereafter, the relation is stable at about zero and continues to the present. The Chattahoochee River at Atlanta, GA (fig. 37), experienced mild aggradation from about 1940 to 1960, followed by stability that has continued to the present. Another station with a dual response is Tobesofkee Creek near Macon, GA (fig. 38). This site was stable until about 1990 when it abruptly began to degrade.

Exploratory analysis of width and discharge was conducted for gages exhibiting large variability in this relation (figs. 13, 14, 22, 35, 36). Width and discharge were plotted for successive 5-year periods to determine if widths had increased over time for specific discharge conditions. This analysis was problematic because of differing discharge measurement locations. For example, in figure 35 what appears to be two distinct groups of width measurements, which could relate to a large change in width, actually represent two different locations used when measuring stream discharge. The lower group resulted from measurements made from the bridge, whereas the upper group resulted from downstream wading locations and historical cableway measurements. Many of the width-discharge plots have outlying data points that appear to be erroneous values (for example, fig. 14). After examining the records, these points often represent a measurement made at a different cross section. Some of the locations have a large difference in the relation between width and discharge, often appearing as a sigmoidal relation. This difference often is due to a change in the control conditions, such as going from low-water control (riffle or bars) to channel control or from channel control to terrace or valley control. Figure 18C represents such a condition, where the channel is the control until bankfull stage (approximately 15 ft or 9,000 cubic feet per second) is reached at which point water spills onto the flood plain and spreads out with increasing discharge until terrace or valley control (at about 800 ft wide) is reached. Because of inconsistent measurement locations, lateral adjustment that could potentially cause changes in the relation between stage and discharge and thus stage-residual trends could not clearly be identified. However, width-discharge plots can aid in bankfull identification as well as indicate general channel shape.

Summary and Conclusions

Data were needed to support a USGS study investigating the effects of altered streamflow conditions on biotic response. As a part of that study, stream-channel stability was assessed to determine if the effects of geomorphic adjustments could mask the effects of altered flow conditions as well as infer the persistence of general habitat conditions. An examination of the residuals of the inverse stage-discharge relation was used to determine channel stability. Once the data had been compiled and corrected, this method provided a fairly simple means of examining channel adjustments independent of discharge. Channel response of the gages analyzed varied. Of the 37 streamgaging stations analyzed, 11 demonstrated a degrading trend while only 6 showed an aggrading trend. Both of these trends are inferred from trends in water-surface elevation. Fourteen of the gages showed considerable stability with only moderate adjustments. Of the remaining six gages, three illustrated wavy patterns while the others demonstrated a dual response of degrading to stable, aggrading to stable, or stable to degrading.

Because residual analysis relies on data generated from the discharge rating, other aspects of the continuity equation must be considered when interpreting adjustments. This form of analysis offers a fairly simple method of viewing the overall picture of channel adjustments. However, further analysis would need to be conducted to determine the actual boundary or flow parameter (velocity) that is responsible for the observed adjustment.

References Cited

Hughes, W.B., Freeman, M.C., Gregory, M.B., and Peterson, J.T., 2007, Water availability for ecological needs in the upper Flint River basin, Georgia—A USGS Science Thrust project: Proceedings of the 2007 Georgia Water Resources Conference, March 27–29, 2007, Athens, Georgia, accessed June 12, 2009, at *http://cms.ce.gatech.edu/gwri/uploads/proceedings/2007/6.6.1.pdf.*

Jacobson, R.B., 1995, Spatial controls on patterns of land-use induced stream disturbances at the drainage-basin scale—An example for gravel-bed streams in the Ozark Plateaus, Missouri, *in* Costa, J.E., Miller, A.J., Potter, K.W., and Wilcock, P.R., eds., Natural and anthropogenic influences in fluvial geomorphology: American Geophysical Union Monograph 89, p. 219–239.

James, L.A., 1991, Incision and morphological evolution of an alluvial channel recovering from hydraulic gold mining sediment: Geological Society of America Bulletin 103, p. 723–736.

Juracek, K.E., and Fitzpatrick, F.A., 2009, Geomorphic applications of stream-gage information: River Research and Applications, v. 25, p. 329–347.

Knighton, D., 1998, Fluvial forms and processes: A new perspective: New York, Oxford University Press, p. 168.

Richard, G.A., Julien, P.Y., and Baird, J.C, 2005, Statistical analysis of lateral migration of the Rio Grande, New Mexico: Geomorphology, v. 71, issues 1–2, p. 139–155.

Schumm, S.A., 1991, To interpret the Earth: Ten ways to be wrong: Cambridge University Press, p. 133.

Simon, A., and Rinaldi, M., 2006, Disturbance, stream incision, and channel evolution: The roles of excess transport capacity and boundary materials in controlling channel response: Geomorphology, v. 79, issues 3–4, p. 361–383.

Smelser, M.G., and Schmidt J.C., 1998, An assessment methodology for determining historical changes in mountain streams: U.S. Department of Agriculture, Forest Service, Rocky Mountain Research Station, Fort Collins, CO, General Technical Report RMRS-GTR-6, p. 29.

Wolman, M.G., 1967, A cycle of sedimentation and erosion in urban river channels: Geografiska Annaler, v. 49A, no. 2–4, p. 385–395.

Figures 2–38

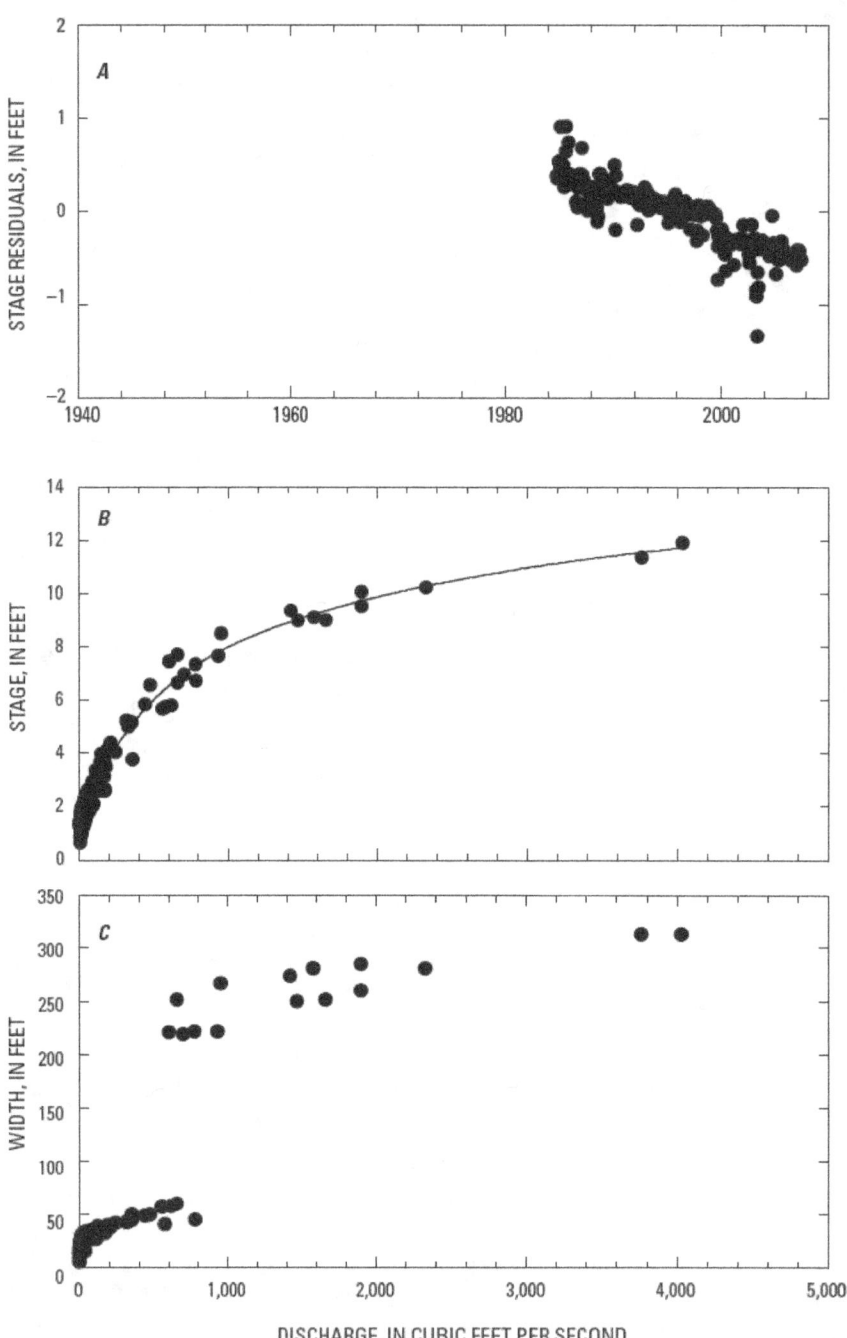

Figure 2. Geomorphic analysis of streamgage data for Suwanee Creek at Suwanee, GA (station number 02334885): *(A)* time series of stage residual; *(B)* stage and discharge; and *(C)* width and discharge.

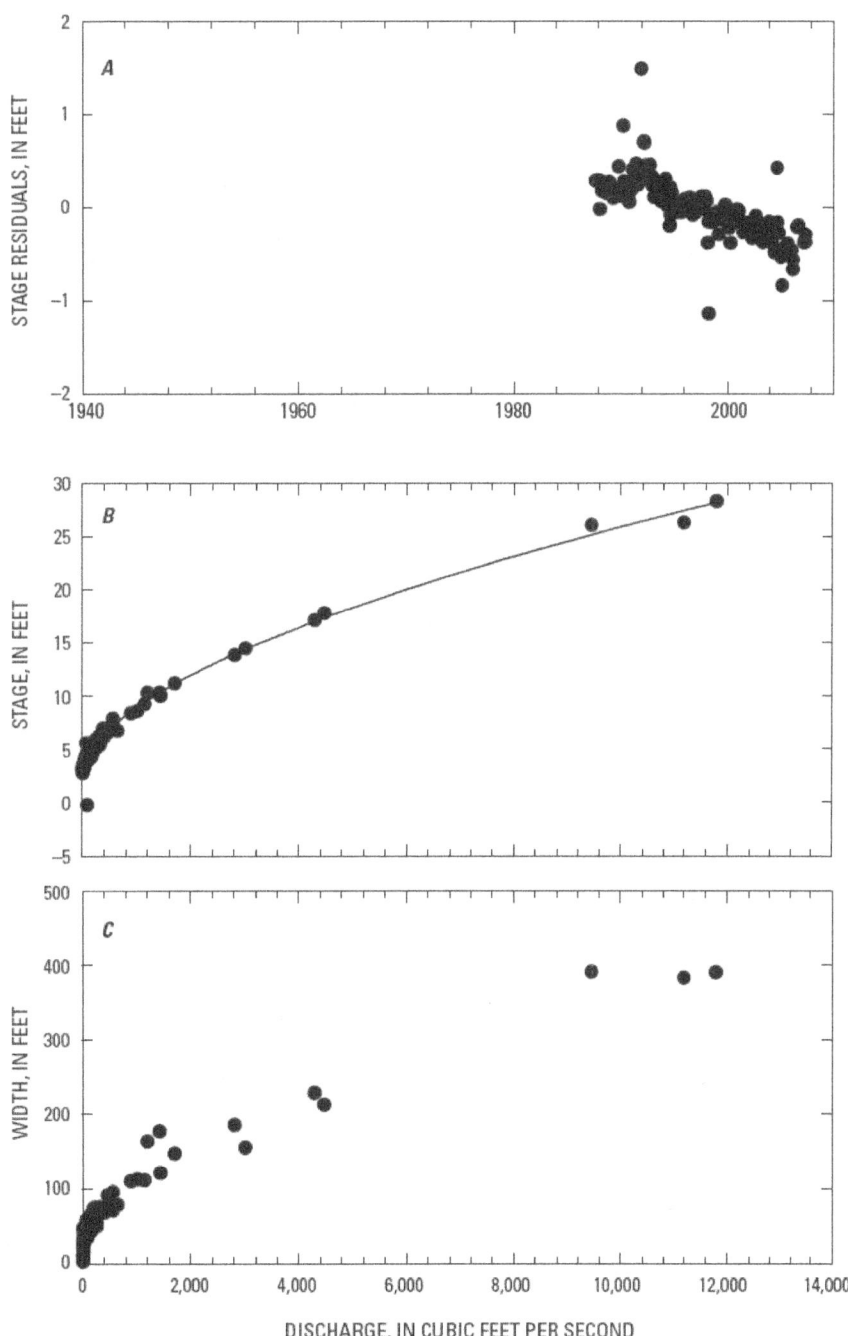

Figure 3. Geomorphic analysis of streamgage data for Little River near Eatonton, GA (station number 02220900): *(A)* time series of stage residuals; *(B)* stage and discharge; and *(C)* width and discharge.

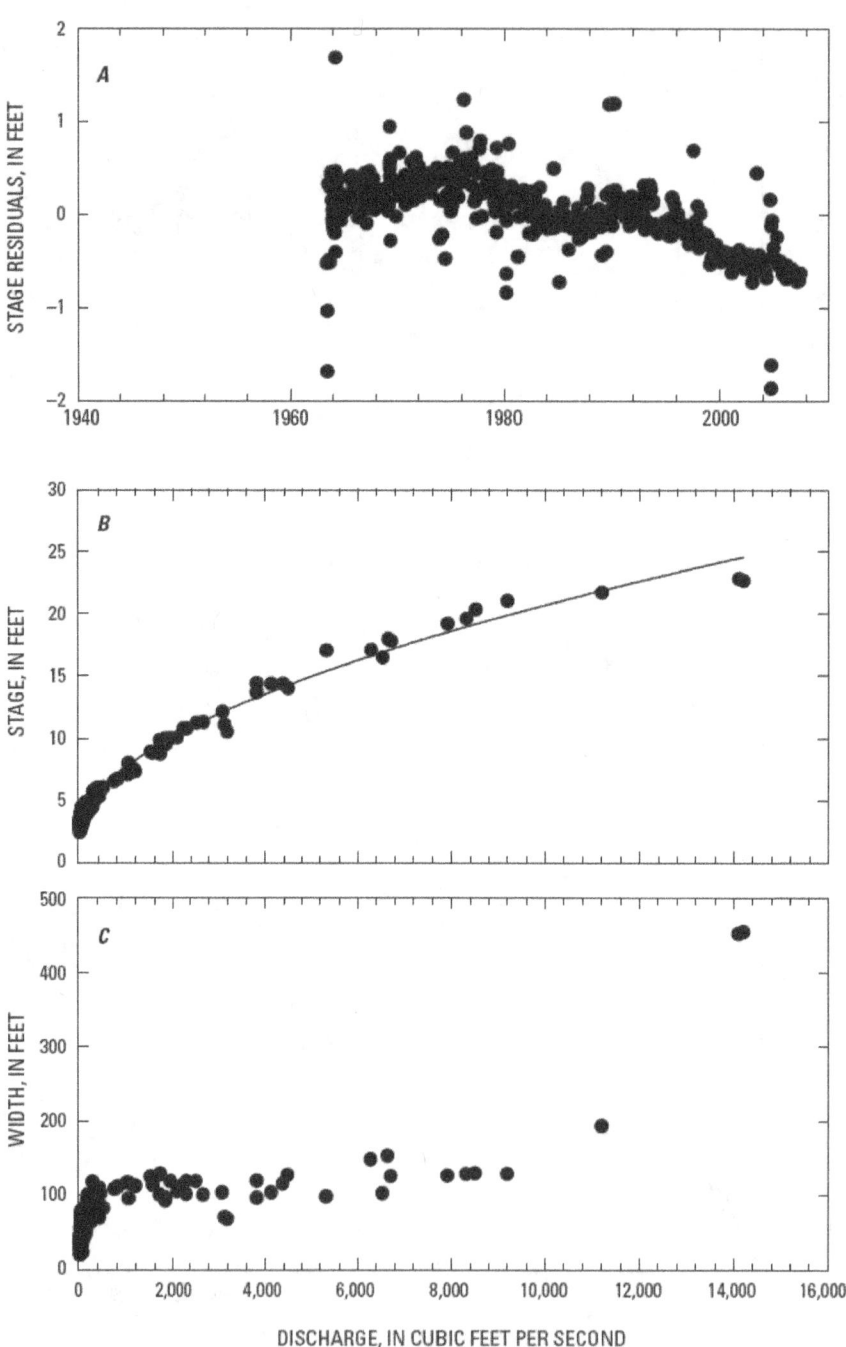

Figure 4. Geomorphic analysis of streamgage data for Peachtree Creek at Atlanta, GA (station number 02336300): *(A)* time series of stage residuals; *(B)* stage and discharge; and *(C)* width and discharge.

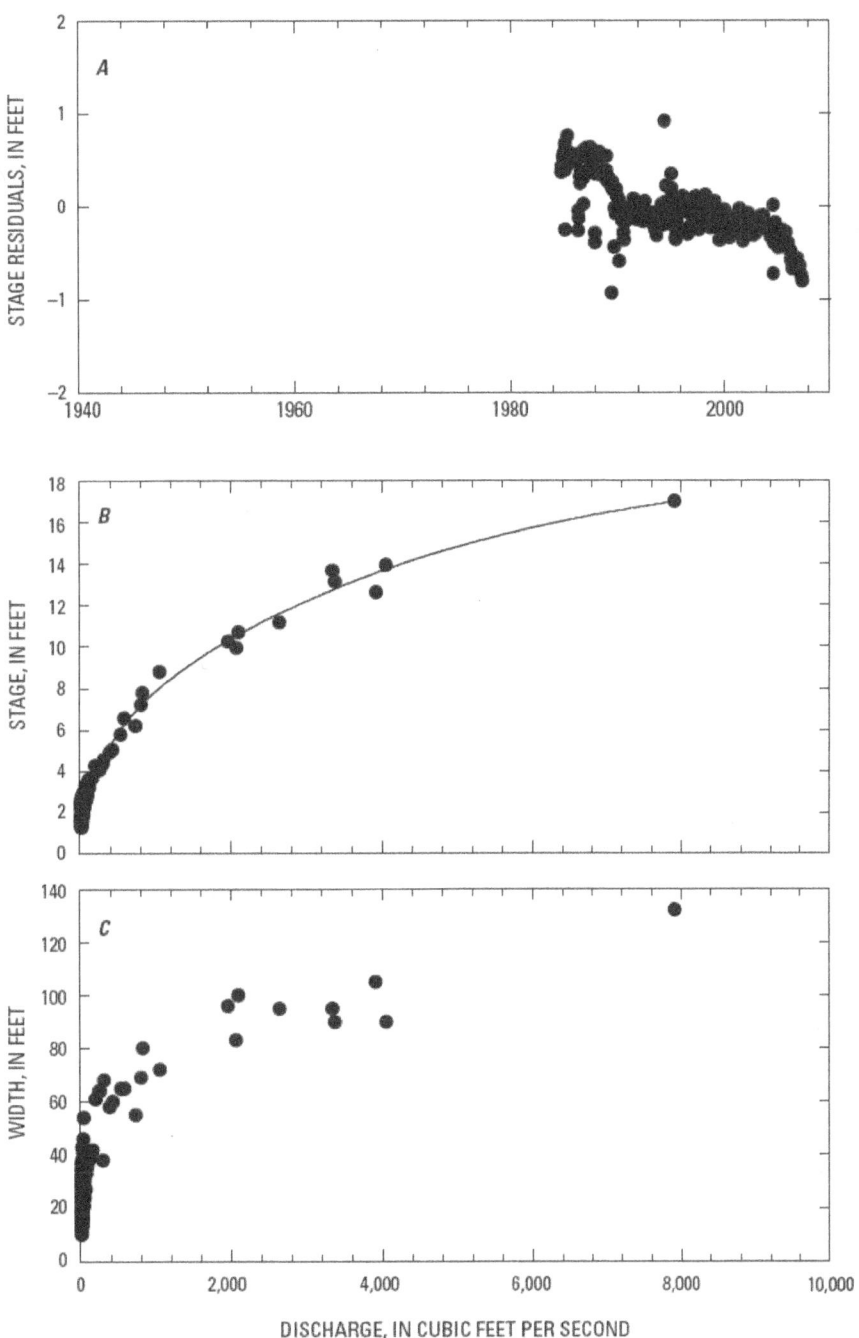

Figure 5. Geomorphic analysis of streamgage data for Sope Creek near Marietta, GA (station number 02335870): *(A)* time series of stage residuals; *(B)* stage and discharge; and *(C)* width and discharge.

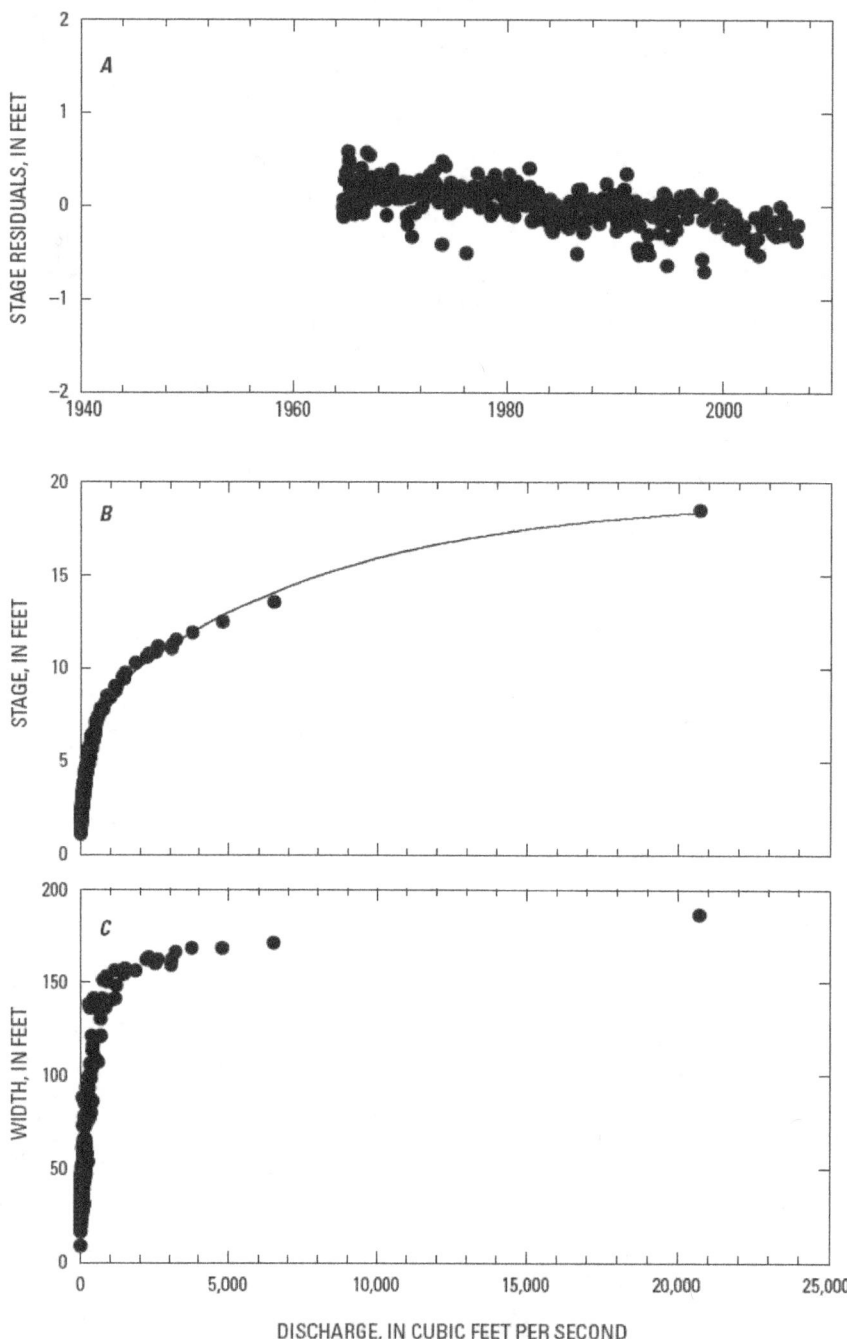

Figure 6.   Geomorphic analysis of streamgage data for Line Creek near Senoia, GA (station number 02344700): *(A)* time series of stage residuals; *(B)* stage and discharge; and *(C)* width and discharge.

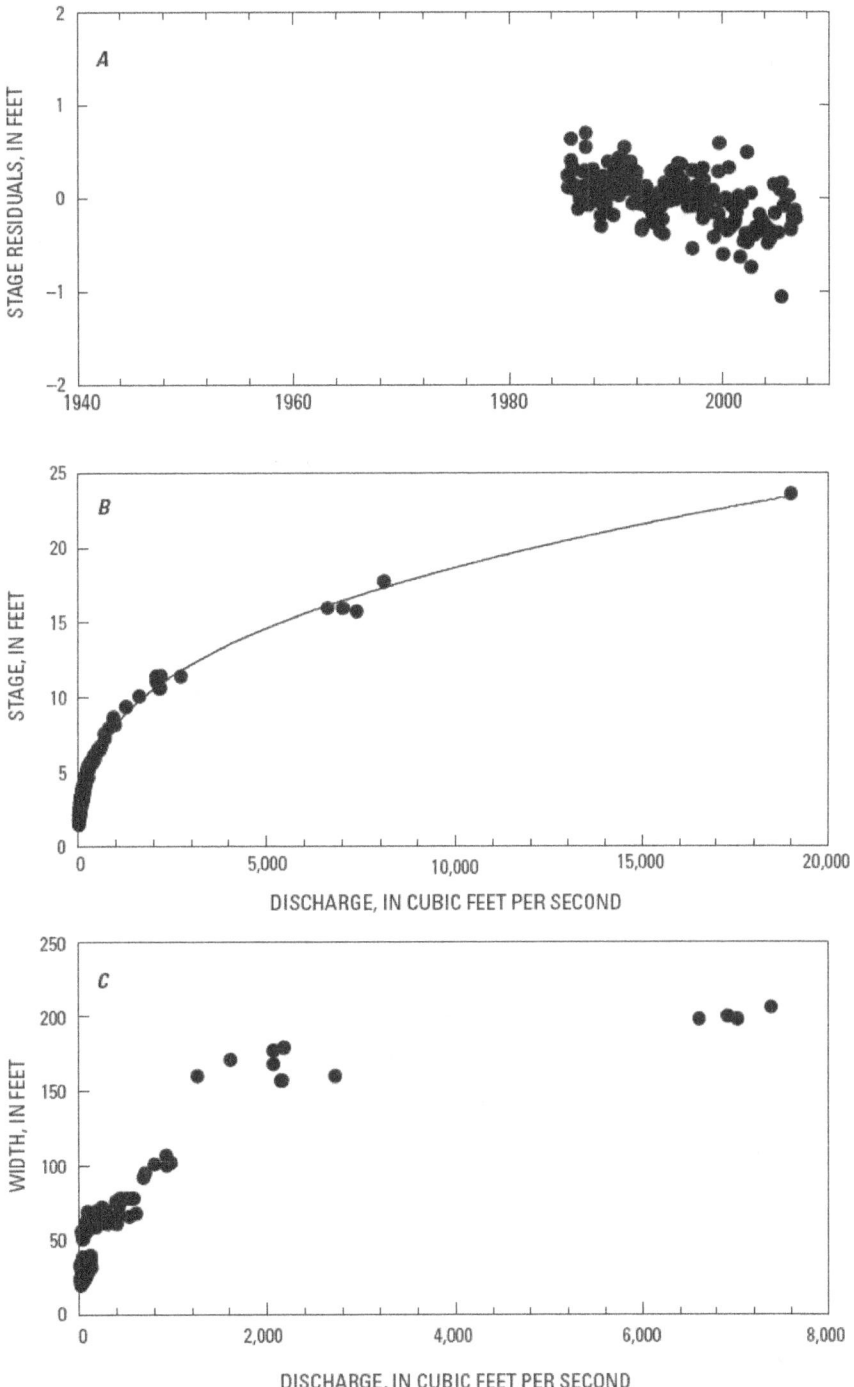

Figure 7.   Geomorphic analysis of streamgage data for Flint River near Lovejoy, GA (station number 02344350): *(A)* time series of stage residuals; *(B)* stage and discharge; and *(C)* width and discharge.

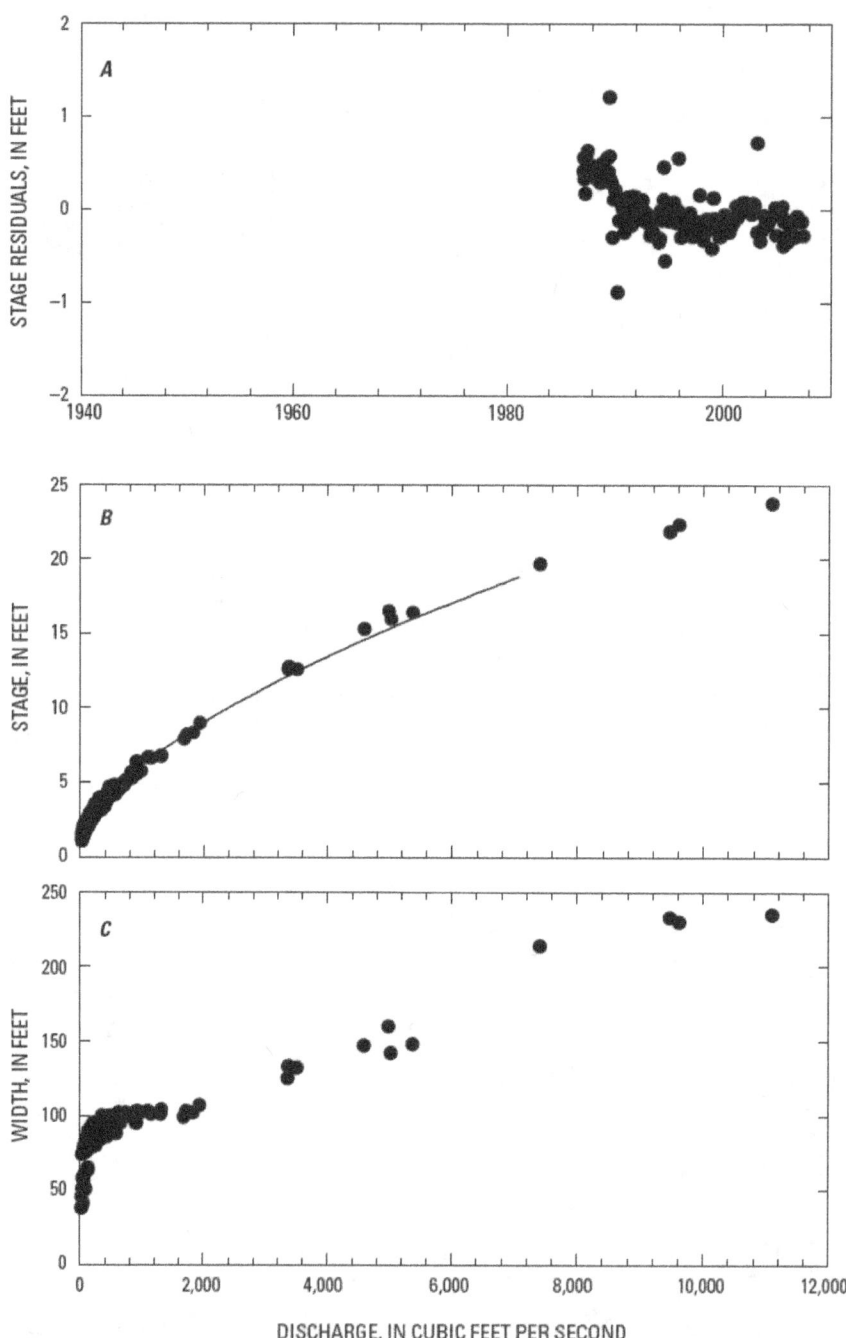

Figure 8. Geomorphic analysis of streamgage data for Middle Oconee River near Arcade, GA (station number 02217475): *(A)* time series of stage residuals; *(B)* stage and discharge; and *(C)* width and discharge.

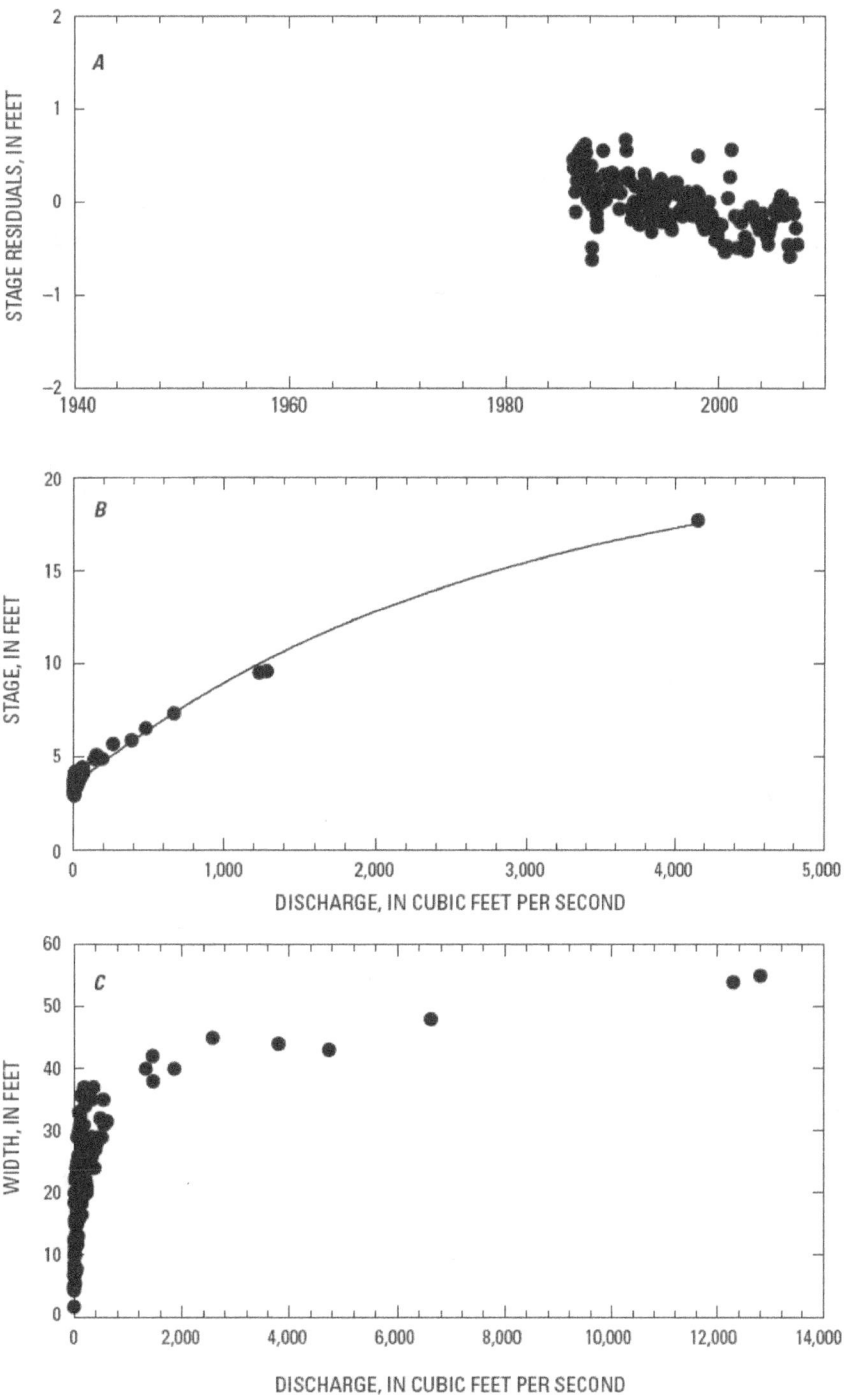

Figure 9. Geomorphic analysis of streamgage data for Kettle Creek near Washington, GA (station number 02193340): *(A)* time series of stage residuals; *(B)* stage and discharge; and *(C)* width and discharge.

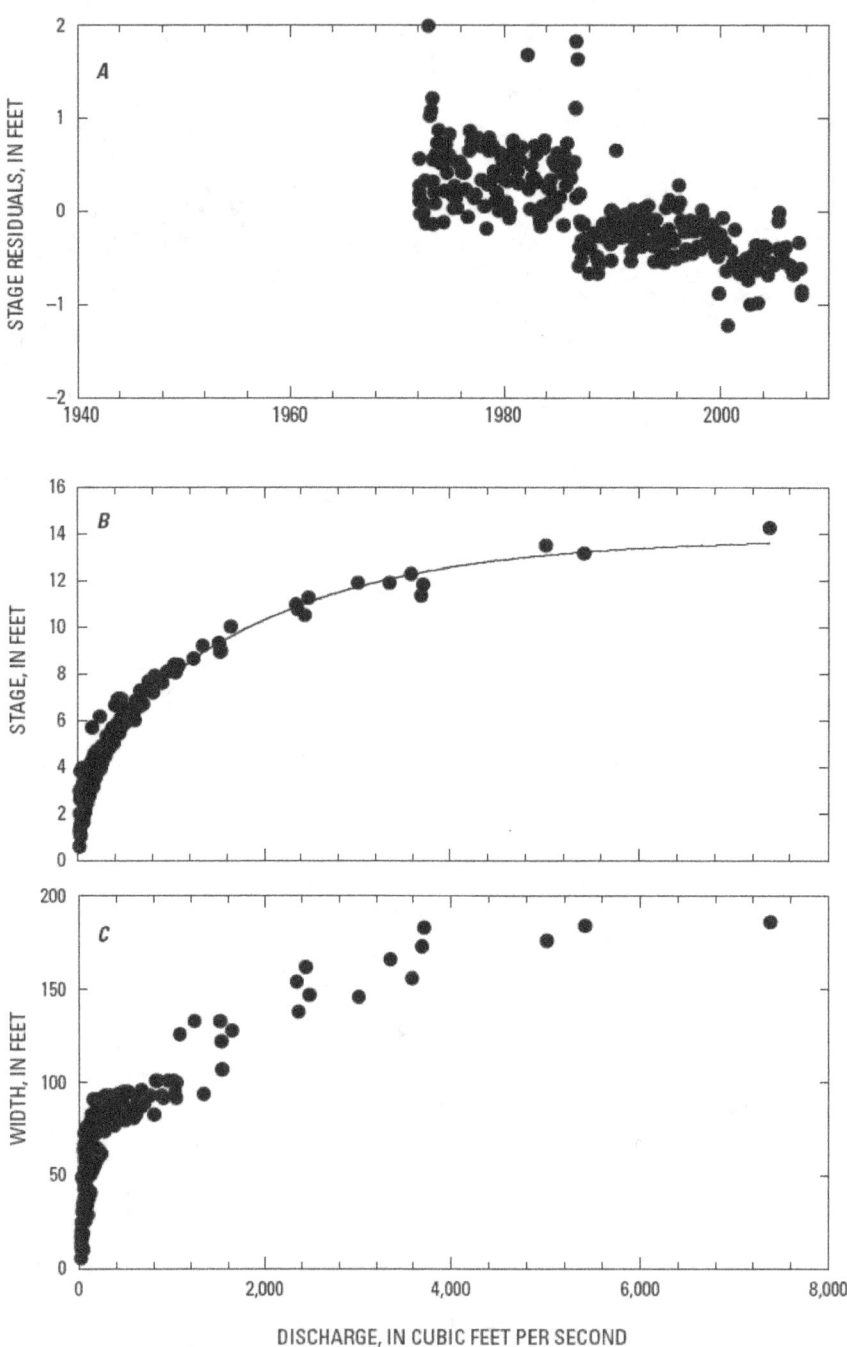

Figure 10.   Geomorphic analysis of streamgage data for Alcovy River above Covington, GA (station number 02208450): *(A)* time series of stage residuals; *(B)* stage and discharge; and *(C)* width and discharge.

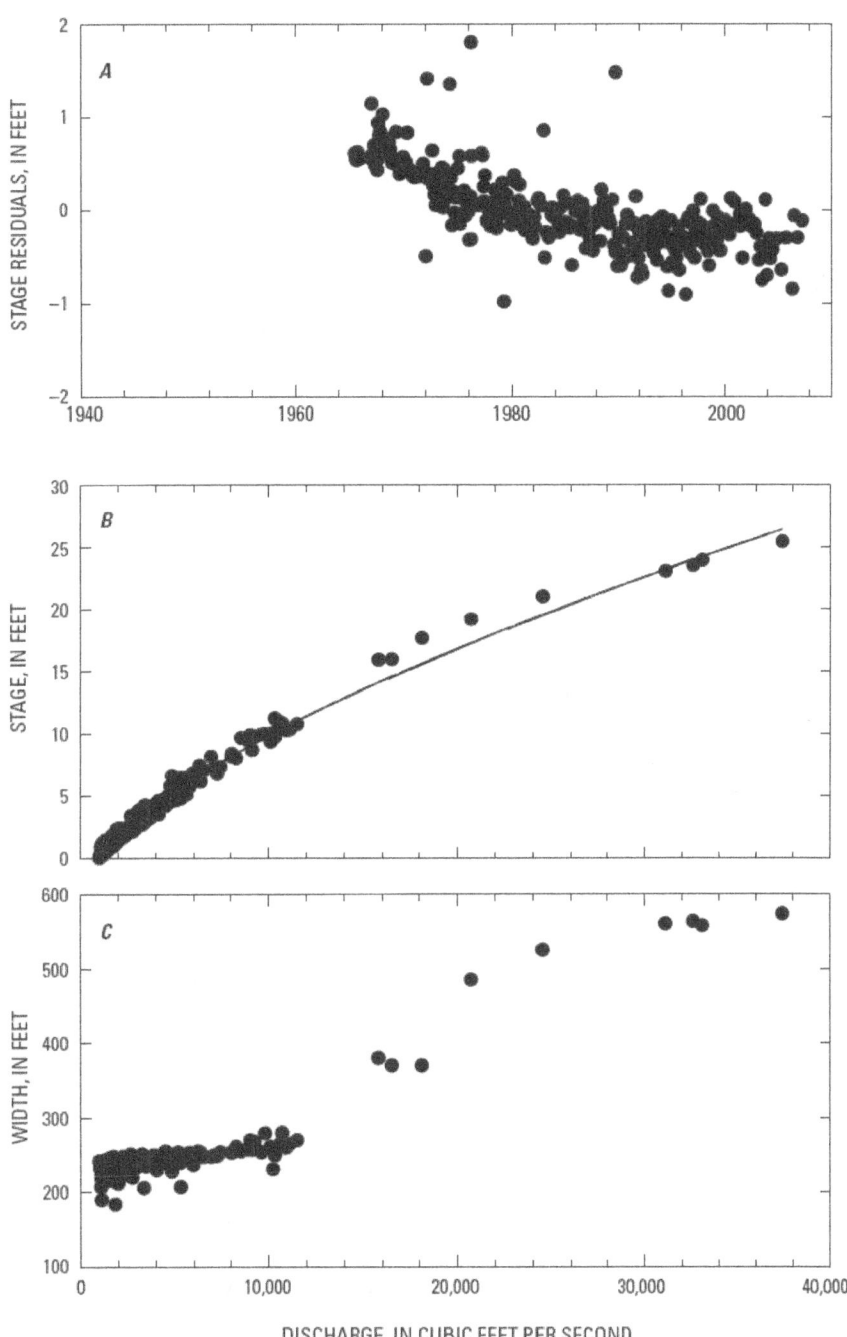

Figure 11. Geomorphic analysis of streamgage data for Chattahoochee River near Fairburn, GA (station number 02337170): *(A)* time series of stage residuals; *(B)* stage and discharge; and *(C)* width and discharge.

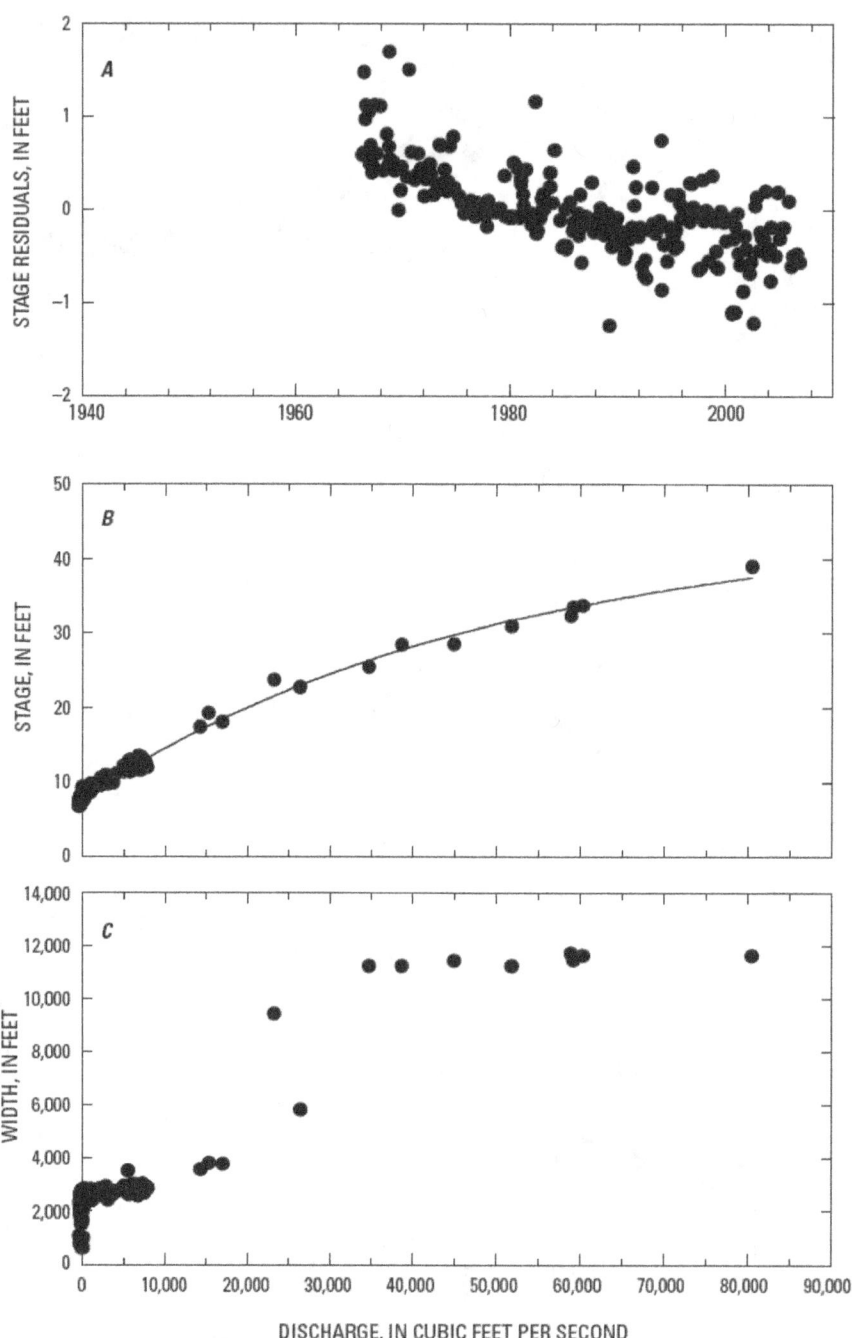

Figure 12.   Geomorphic analysis of streamgage data for Oconee River at Milledgeville, GA (station number 02223000): *(A)* time series of stage residuals; *(B)* stage and discharge; and *(C)* width and discharge.

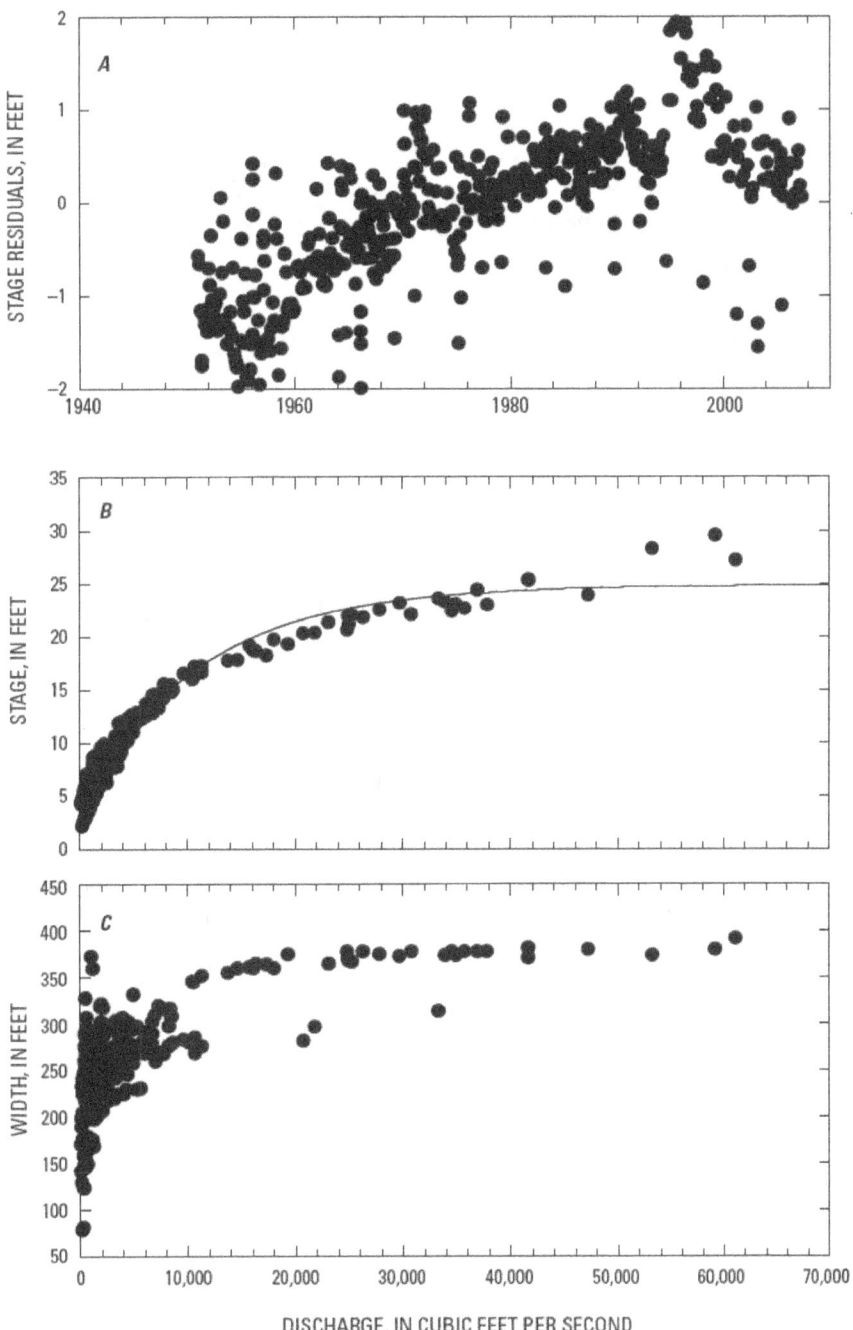

Figure 13. Geomorphic analysis of streamgage data for Ockmulgee River at Macon, GA (station number 02213000): *(A)* time series of stage residuals; *(B)* stage and discharge; and *(C)* width and discharge.

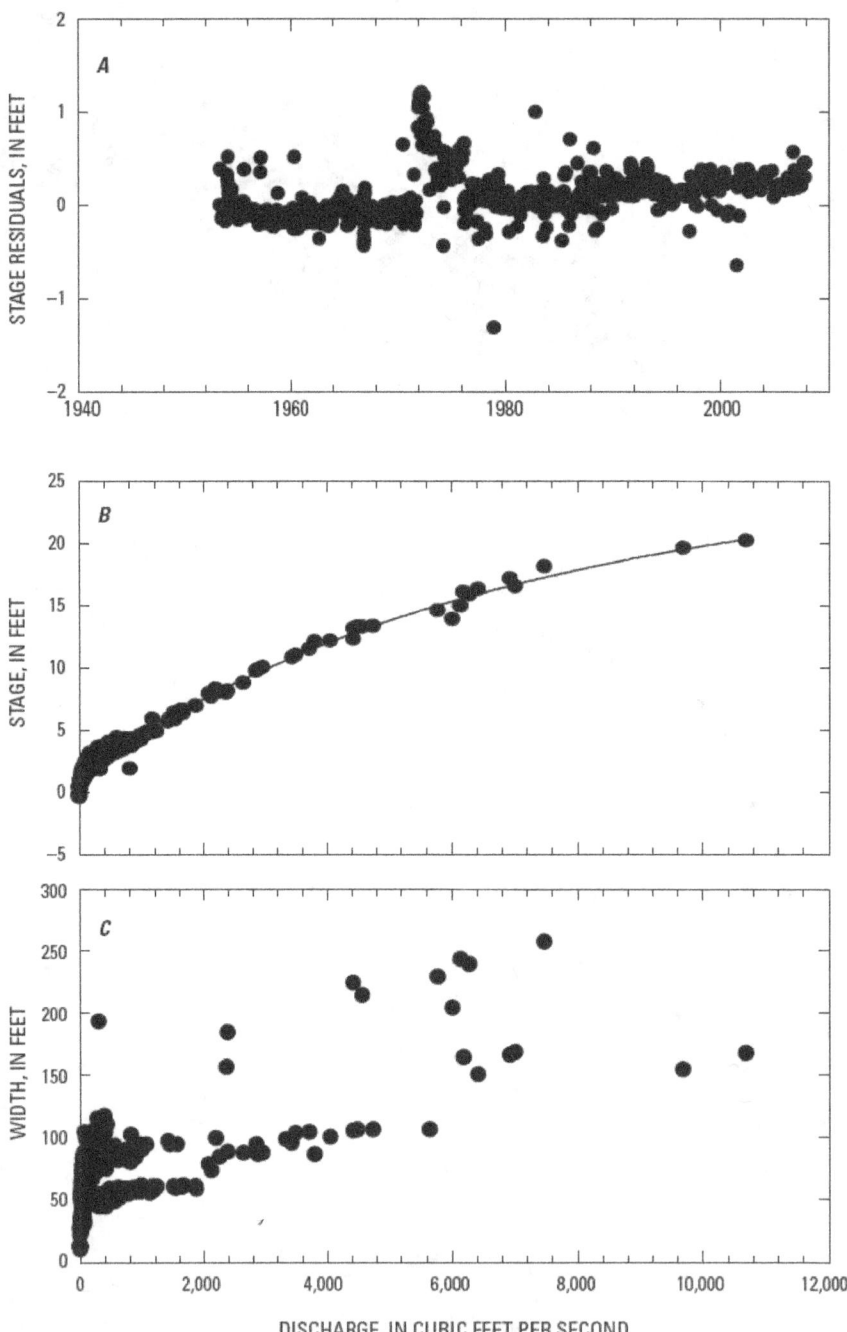

Figure 14.   Geomorphic analysis of streamgage data for Sweetwater Creek near Austell, GA (station number 02337000): *(A)* time series of stage residuals; *(B)* stage and discharge; and *(C)* width and discharge.

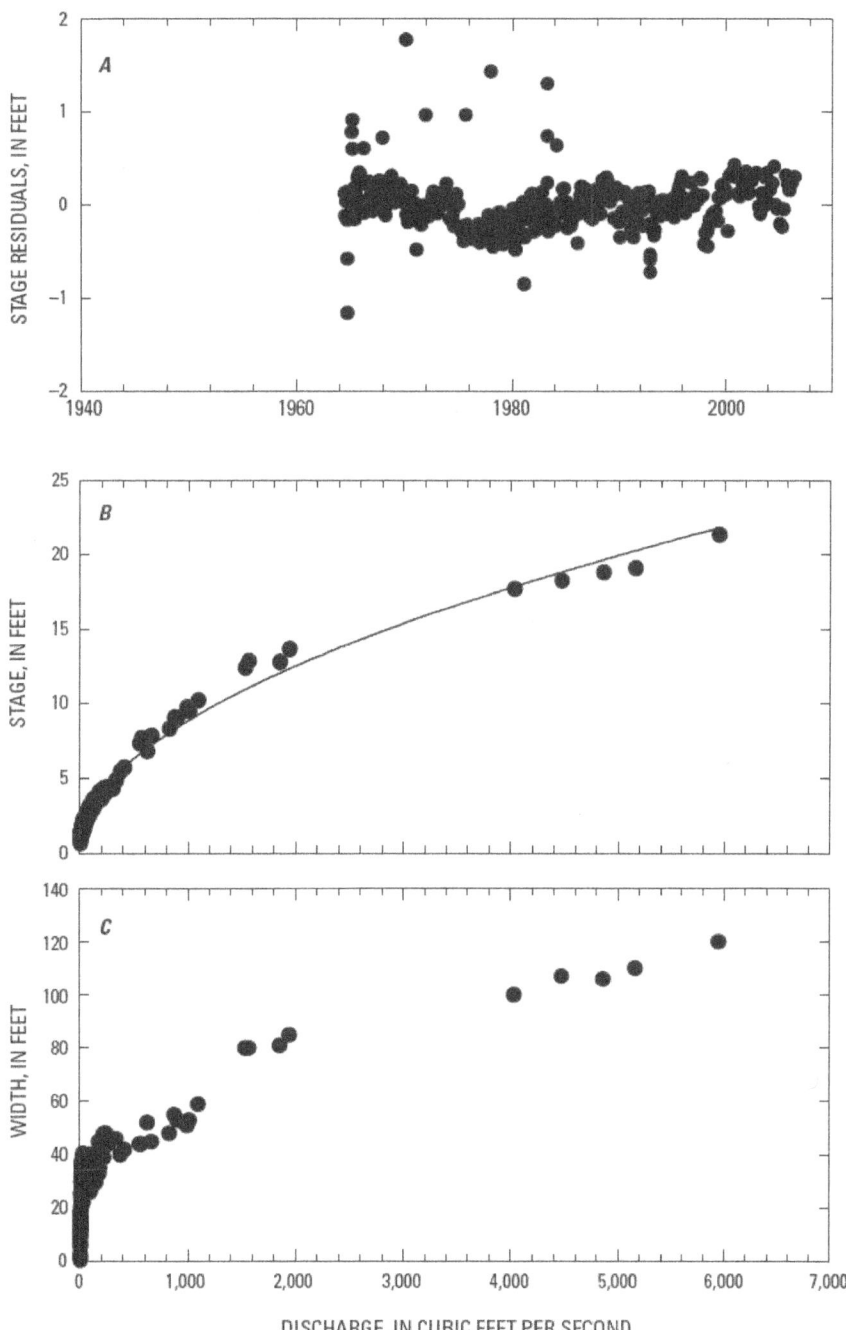

Figure 15. Geomorphic analysis of streamgage data for Falling Creek near Juliette, GA (station number 02212600): *(A)* time series of stage residuals; *(B)* stage and discharge; and *(C)* width and discharge.

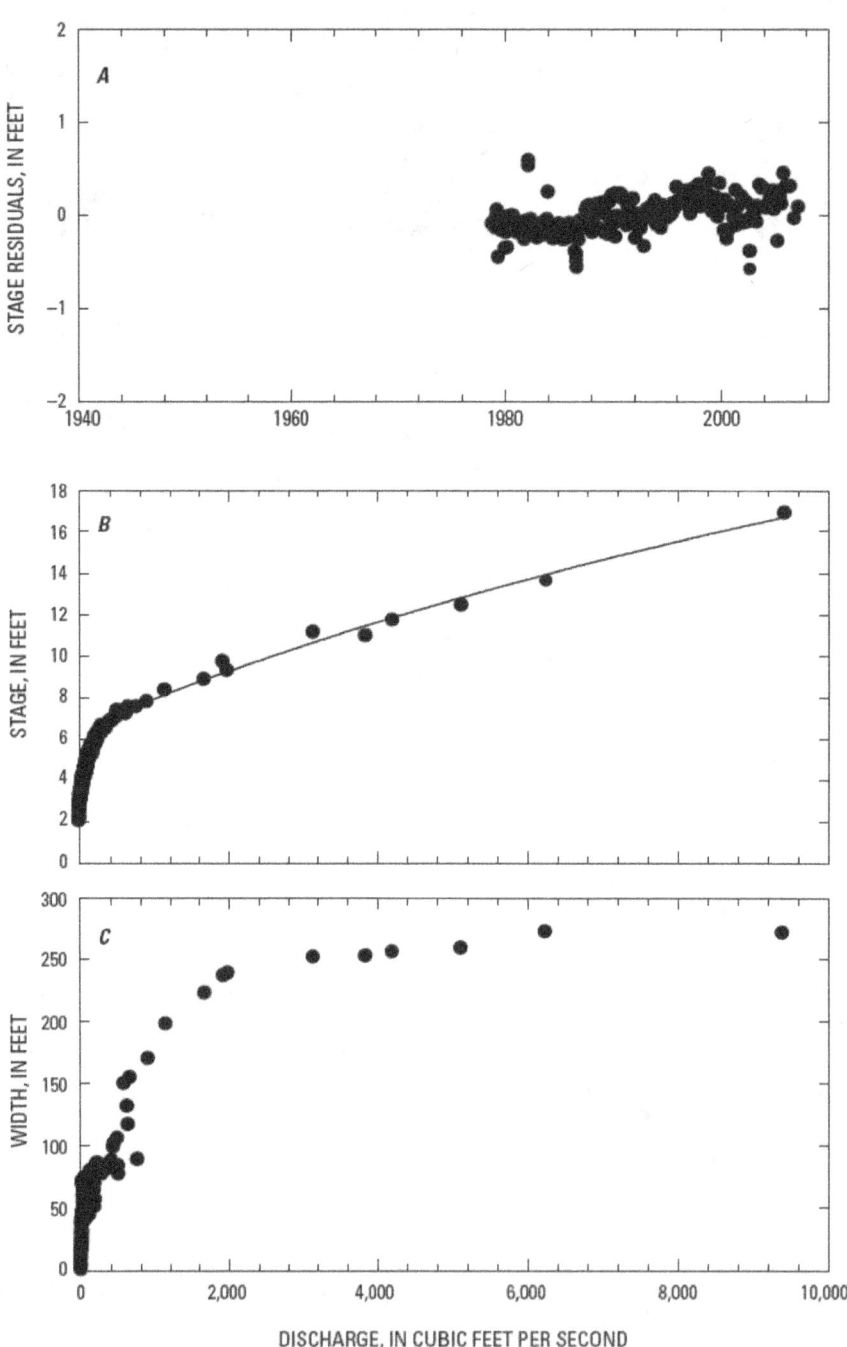

Figure 16.   Geomorphic analysis of streamgage data for New River at GA 100, near Cornith, GA (station number 02338660): *(A)* time series of stage residuals; *(B)* stage and discharge; and *(C)* width and discharge.

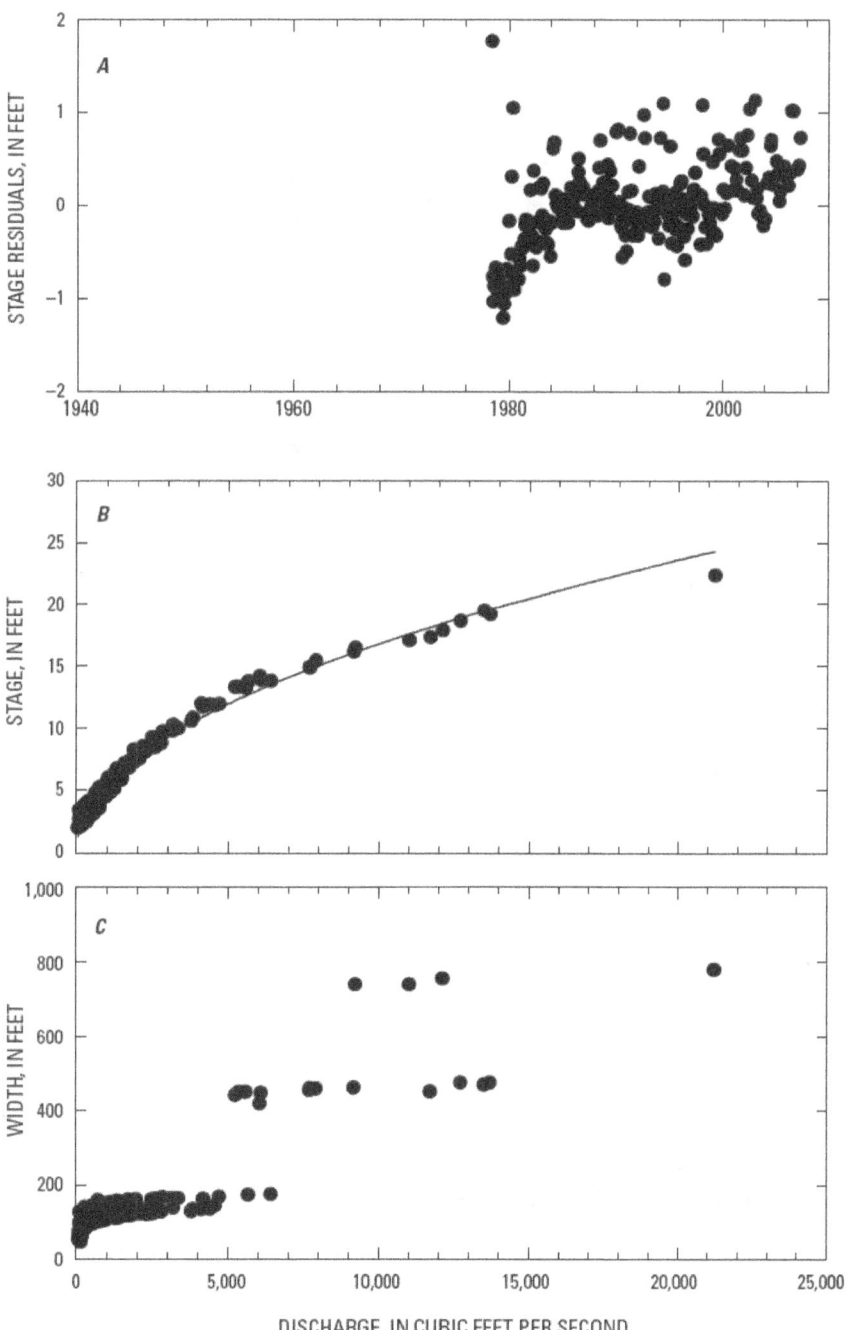

Figure 17. Geomorphic analysis of streamgage data for Oconee River near Penfield, GA (station number 02218300): *(A)* time series of stage residuals; *(B)* stage and discharge; and *(C)* width and discharge.

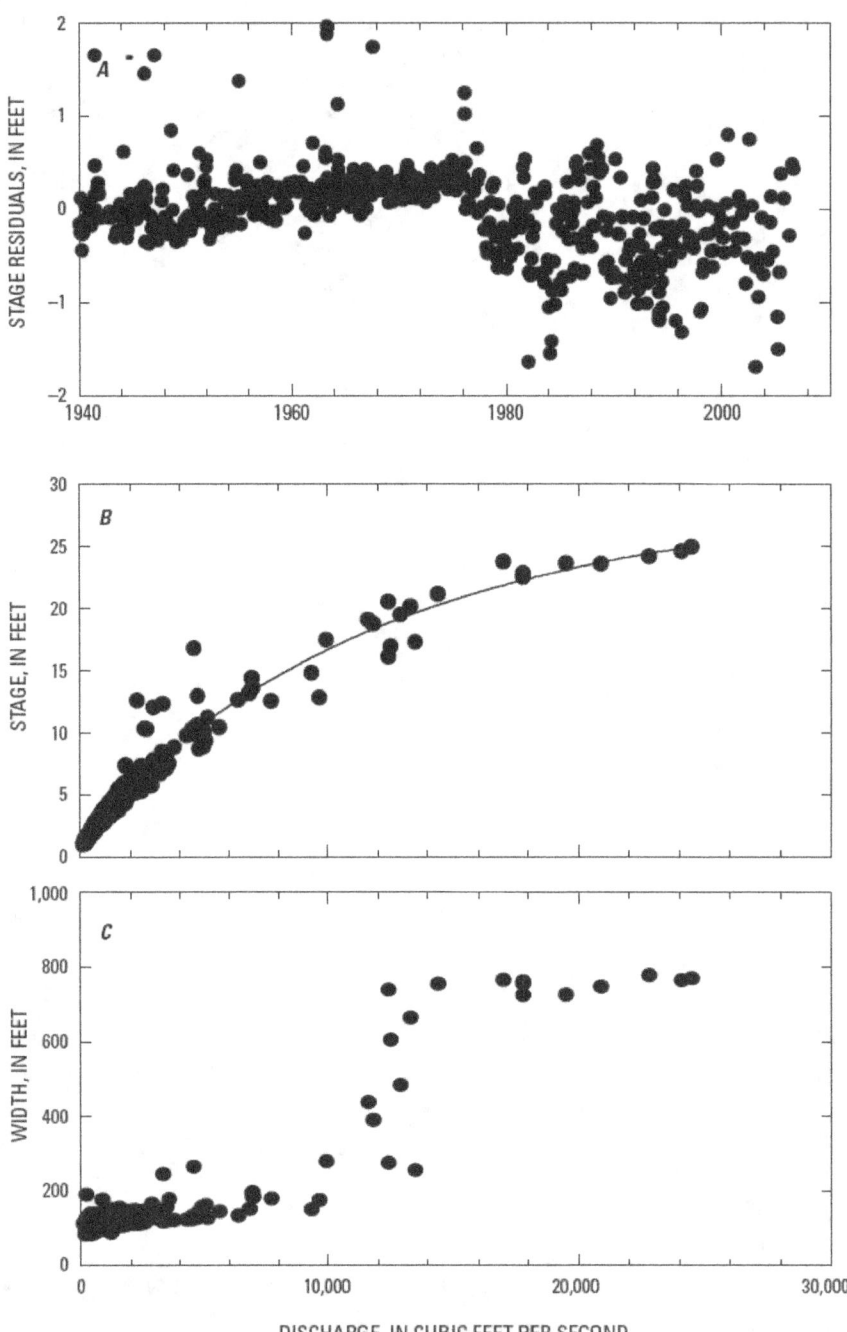

Figure 18.   Geomorphic analysis of streamgage data for Etowah River at Canton, GA (station number 02392000): *(A)* time series of stage residuals; *(B)* stage and discharge; and *(C)* width and discharge.

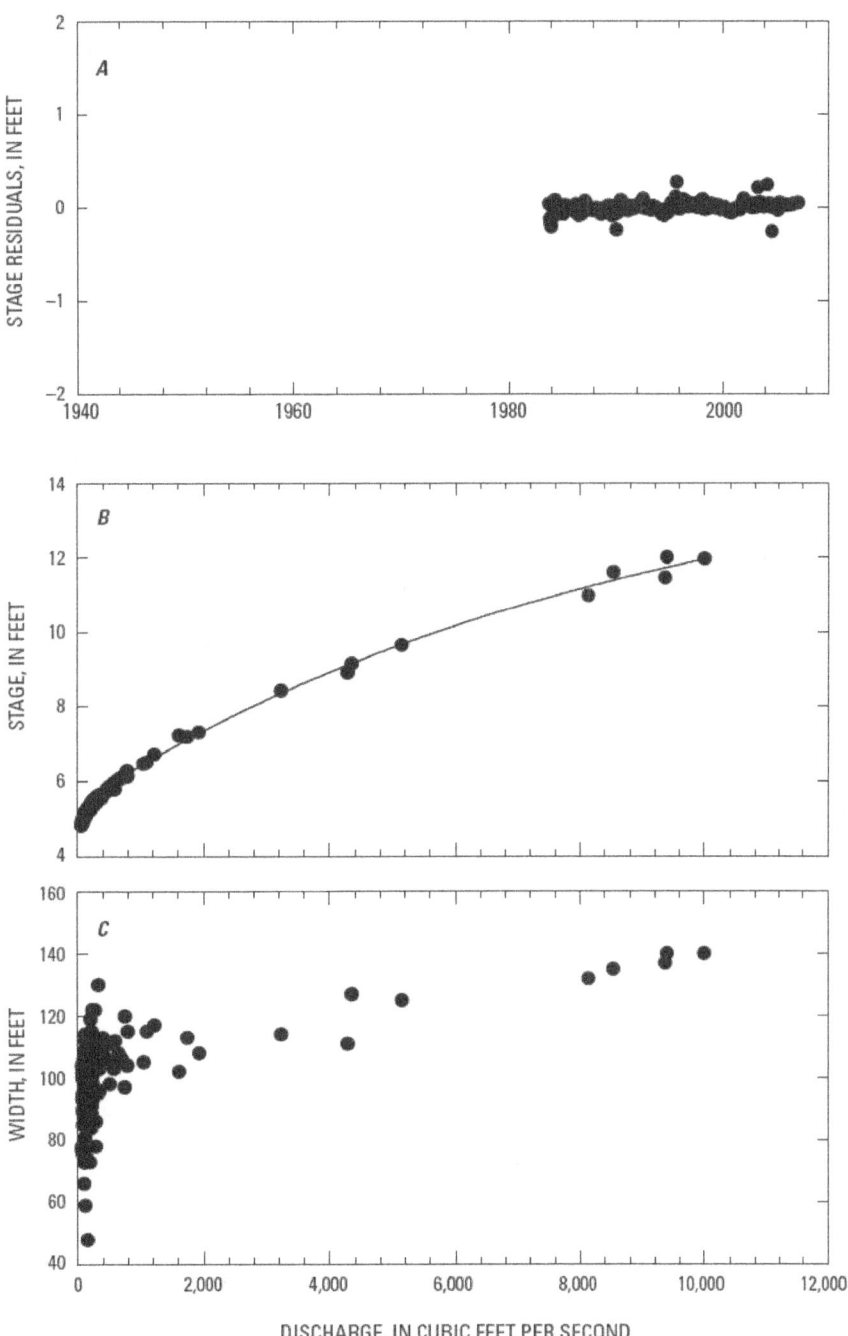

Figure 19. Geomorphic analysis of streamgage data for South River at Klondike Road, near Lithonia, GA (station number 02204070): *(A)* time series of stage residuals; *(B)* stage and discharge; and *(C)* width and discharge.

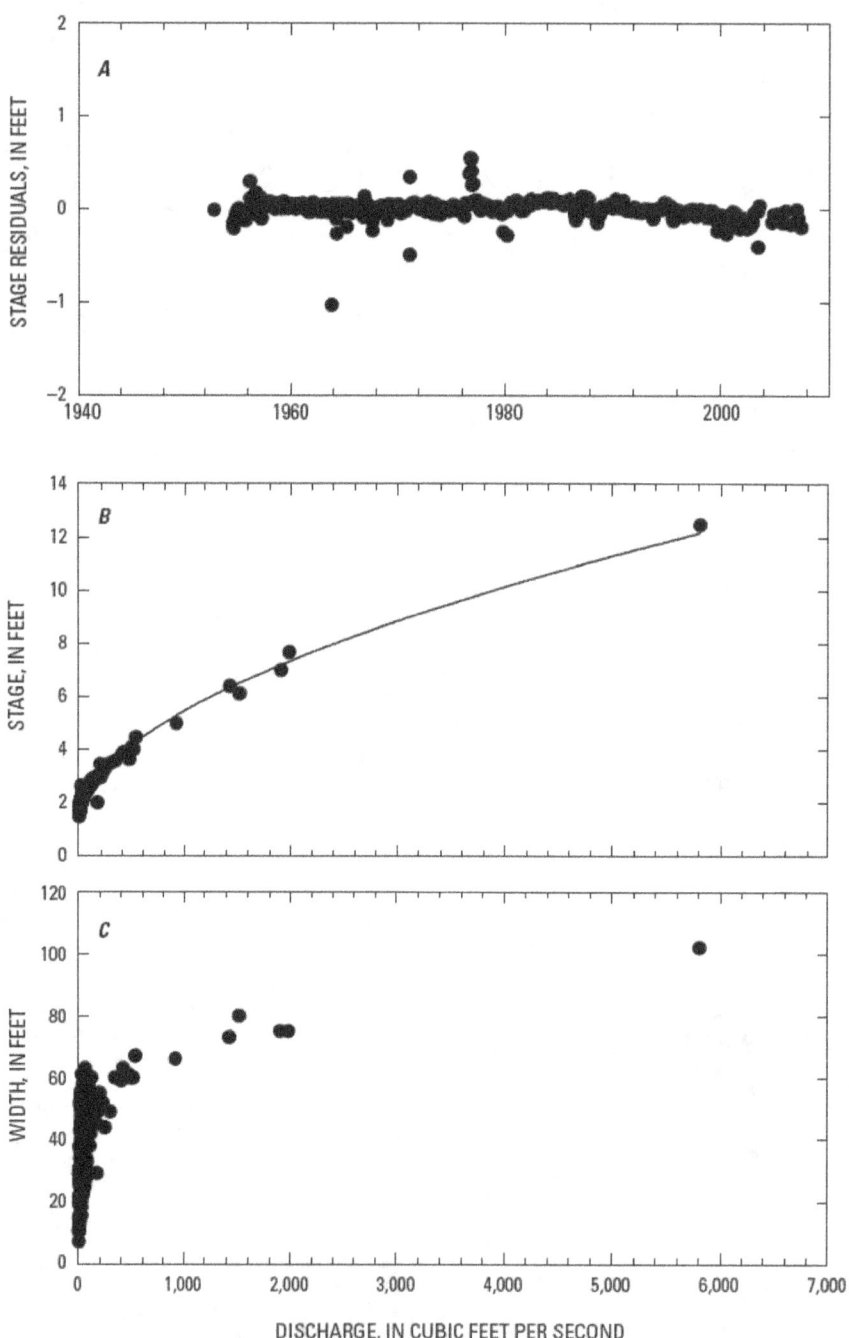

Figure 20.   Geomorphic analysis of streamgage data for Snake Creek near Whitesburg, GA (station number 02337500): *(A)* time series of stage residuals; *(B)* stage and discharge; and *(C)* width and discharge.

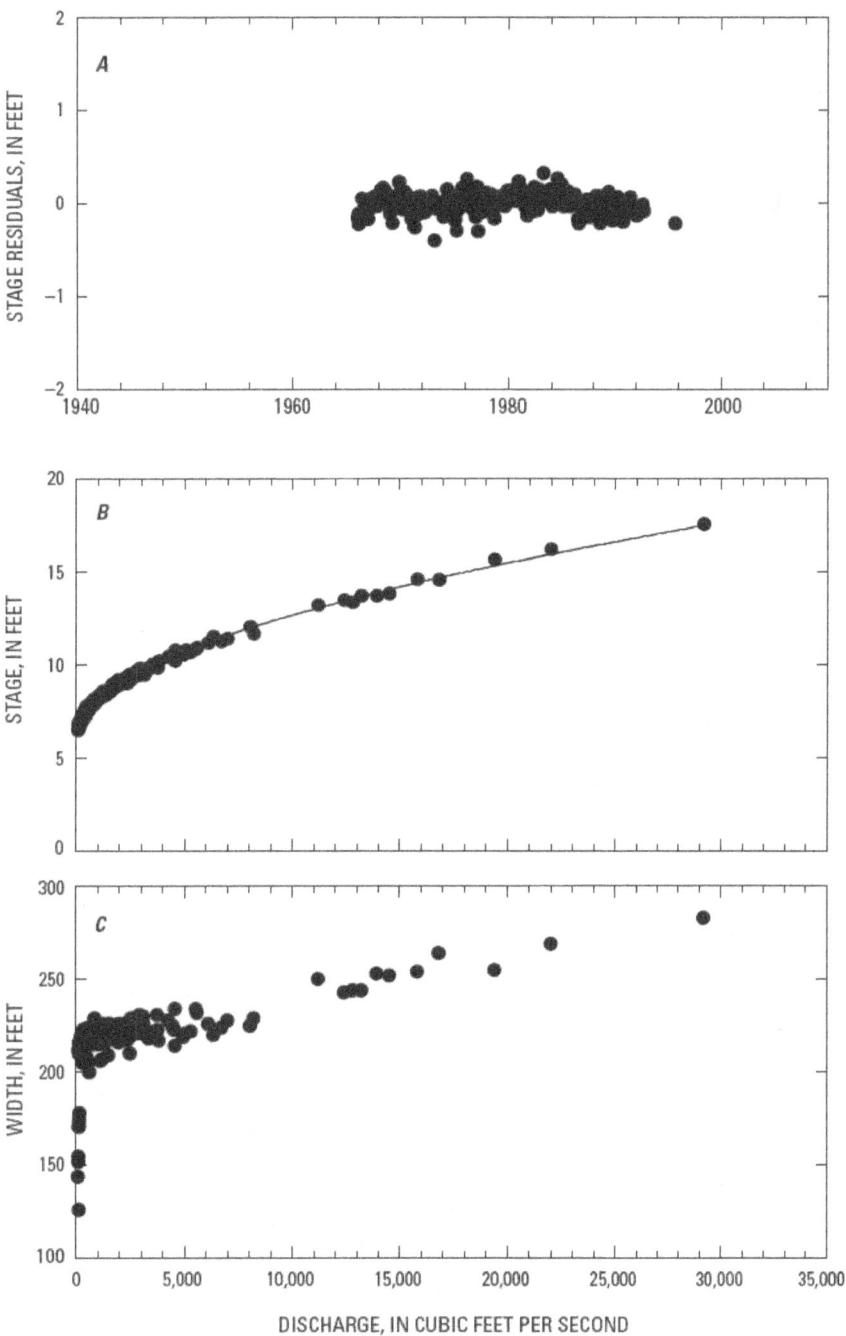

Figure 21. Geomorphic analysis of streamgage data for Flint River near Thomaston, GA (station number 02346180): *(A)* time series of stage residuals; *(B)* stage and discharge; and *(C)* width and discharge.

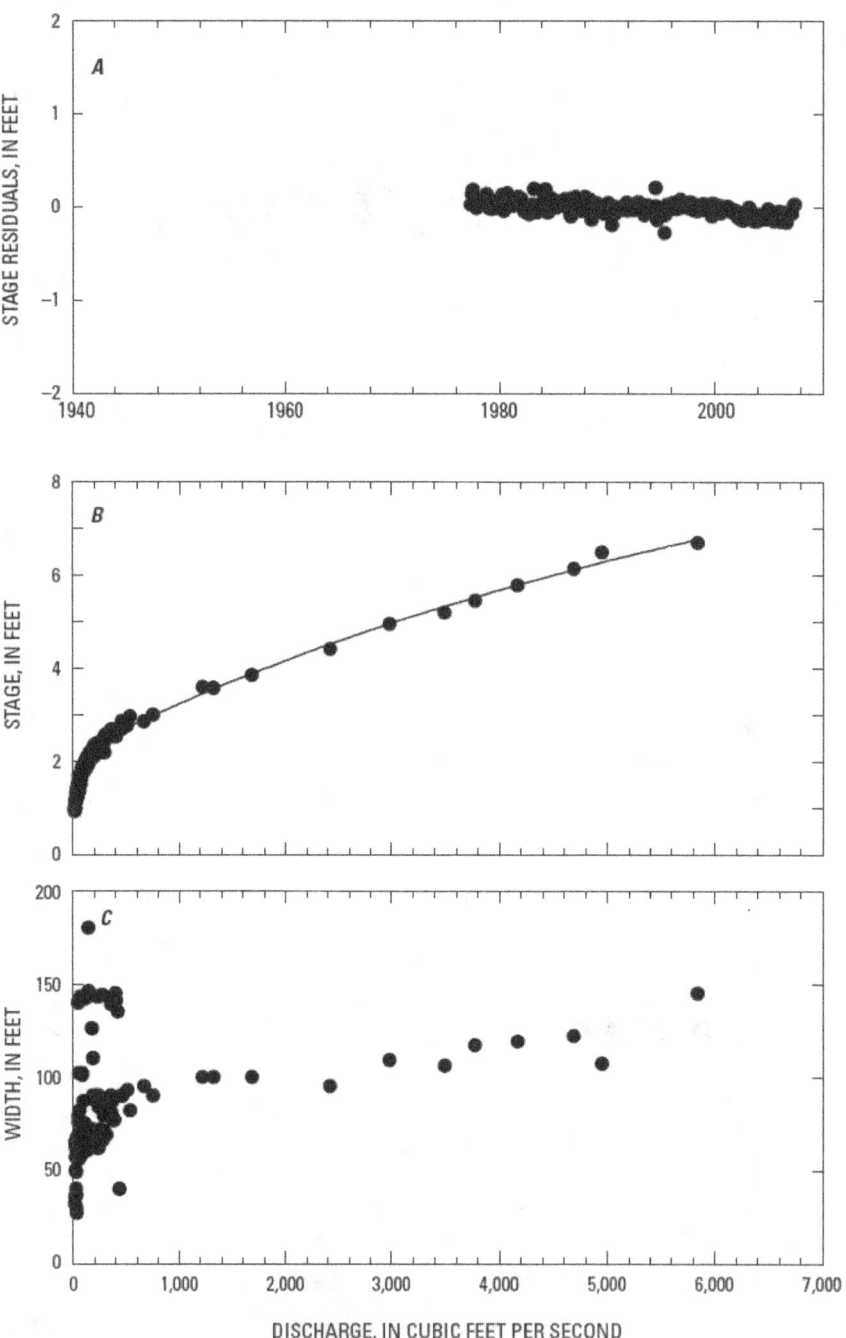

Figure 22.   Geomorphic analysis of streamgage data for Apalachee River near Bostwick, GA (station number 02219000): *(A)* time series of stage residuals; *(B)* stage and discharge; and *(C)* width and discharge.

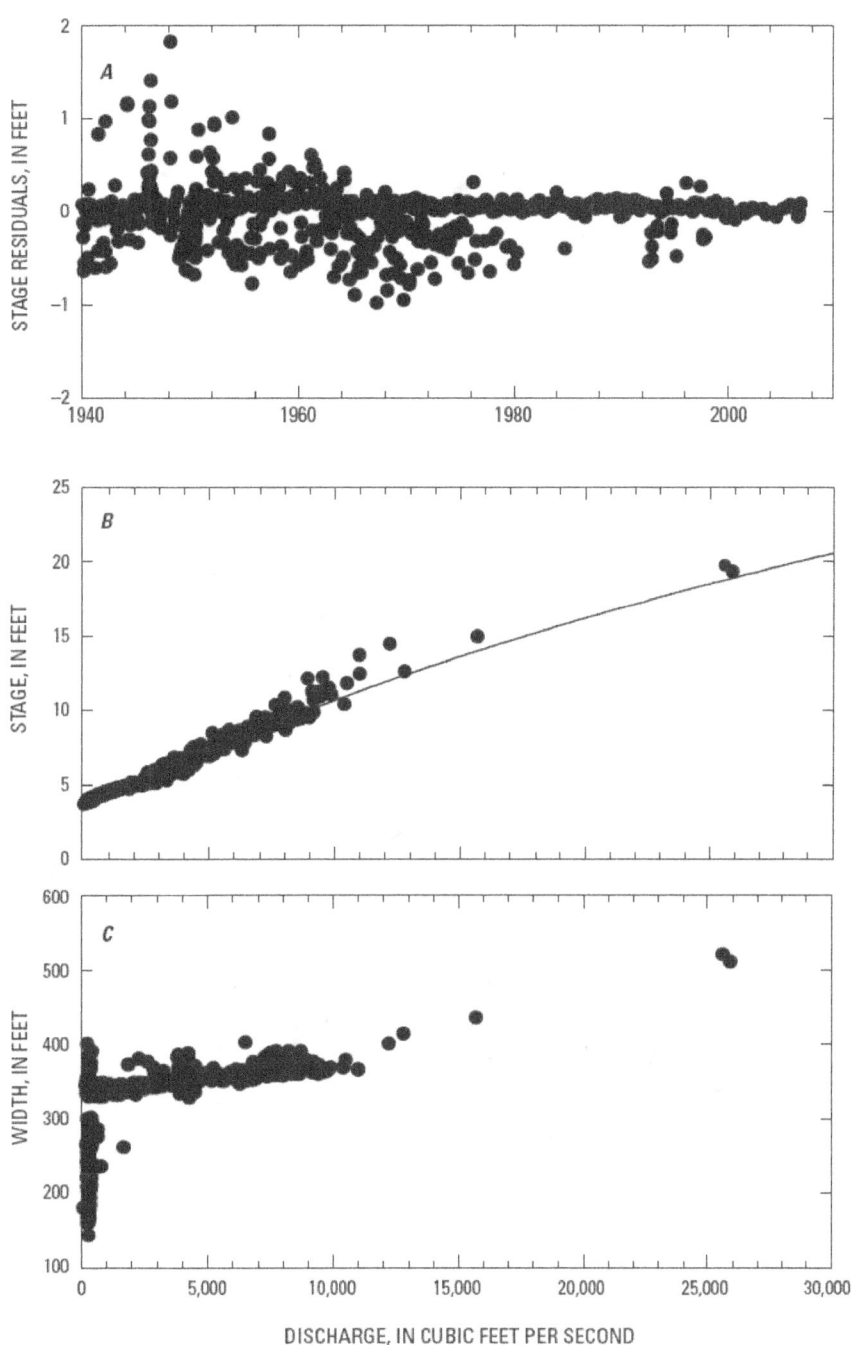

Figure 23. Geomorphic analysis of streamgage data for Etowah River at Allatoona Dam, above Cartersville, GA (station number 02394000): *(A)* time series of stage residuals; *(B)* stage and discharge; and *(C)* width and discharge.

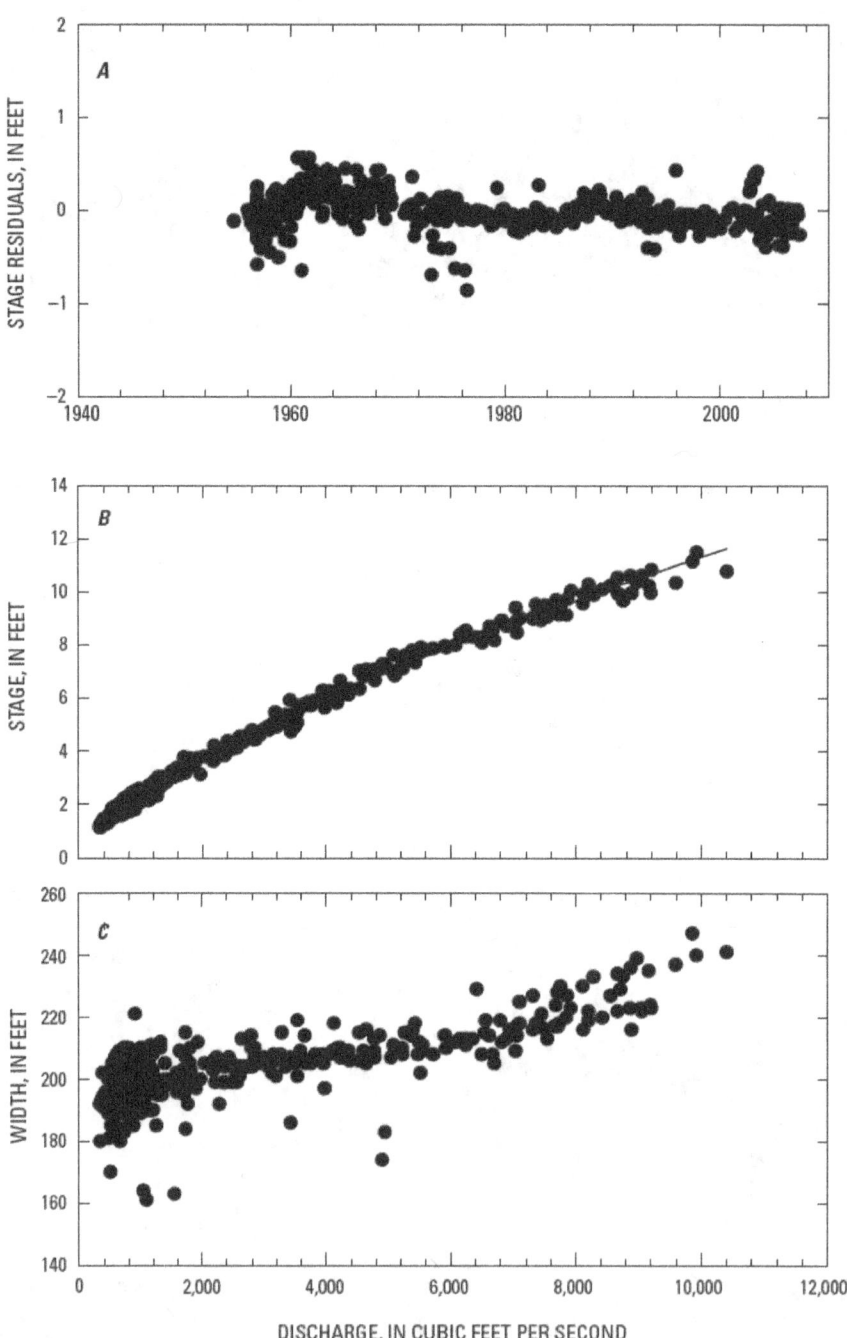

Figure 24. Geomorphic analysis of streamgage data for Chattahoochee River near Norcross, GA (station number 02335000): *(A)* time series of stage residuals; *(B)* stage and discharge; and *(C)* width and discharge.

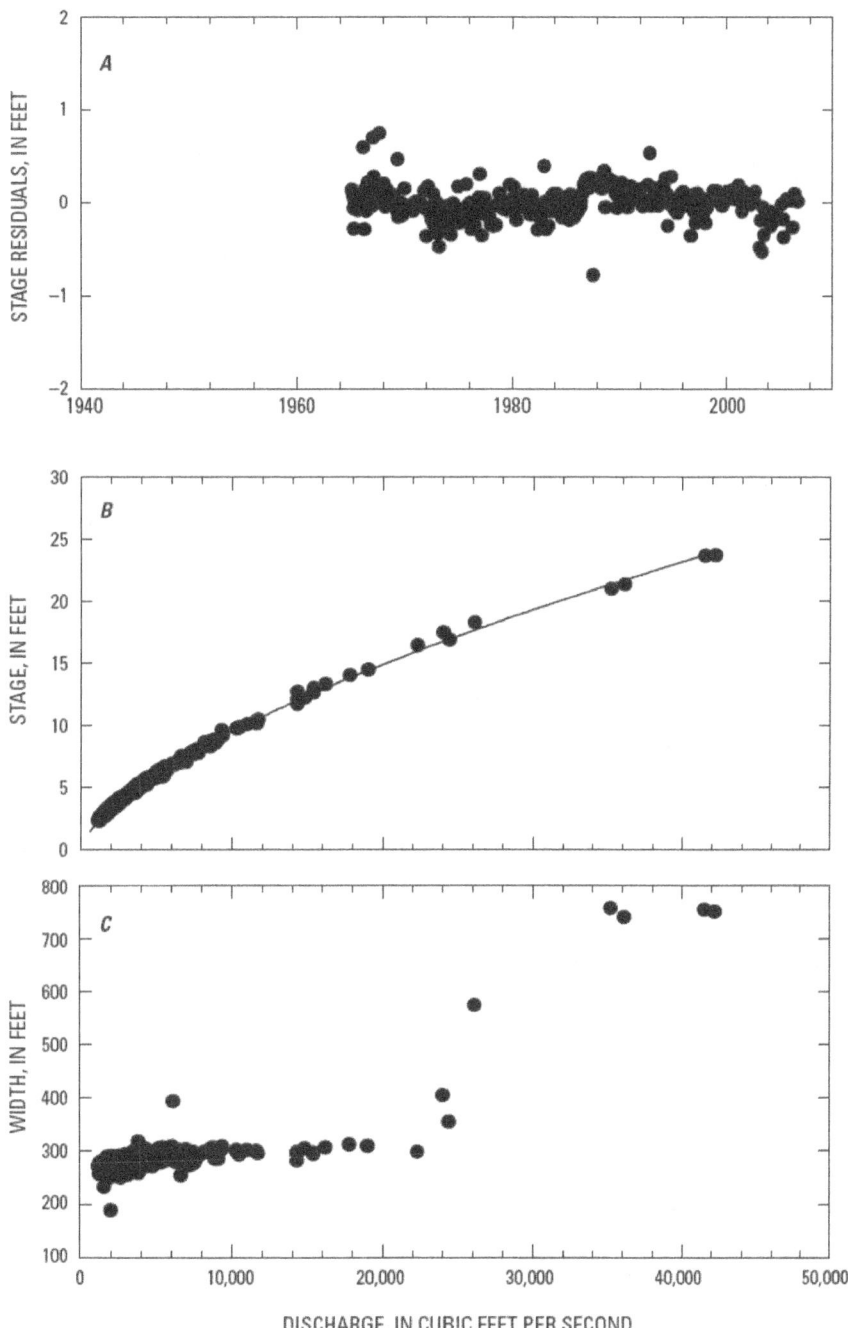

Figure 25. Geomorphic analysis of streamgage data for Chattahoochee River near Whitesburg, GA (station number 02338000): *(A)* time series of stage residuals; *(B)* stage and discharge; and *(C)* width and discharge.

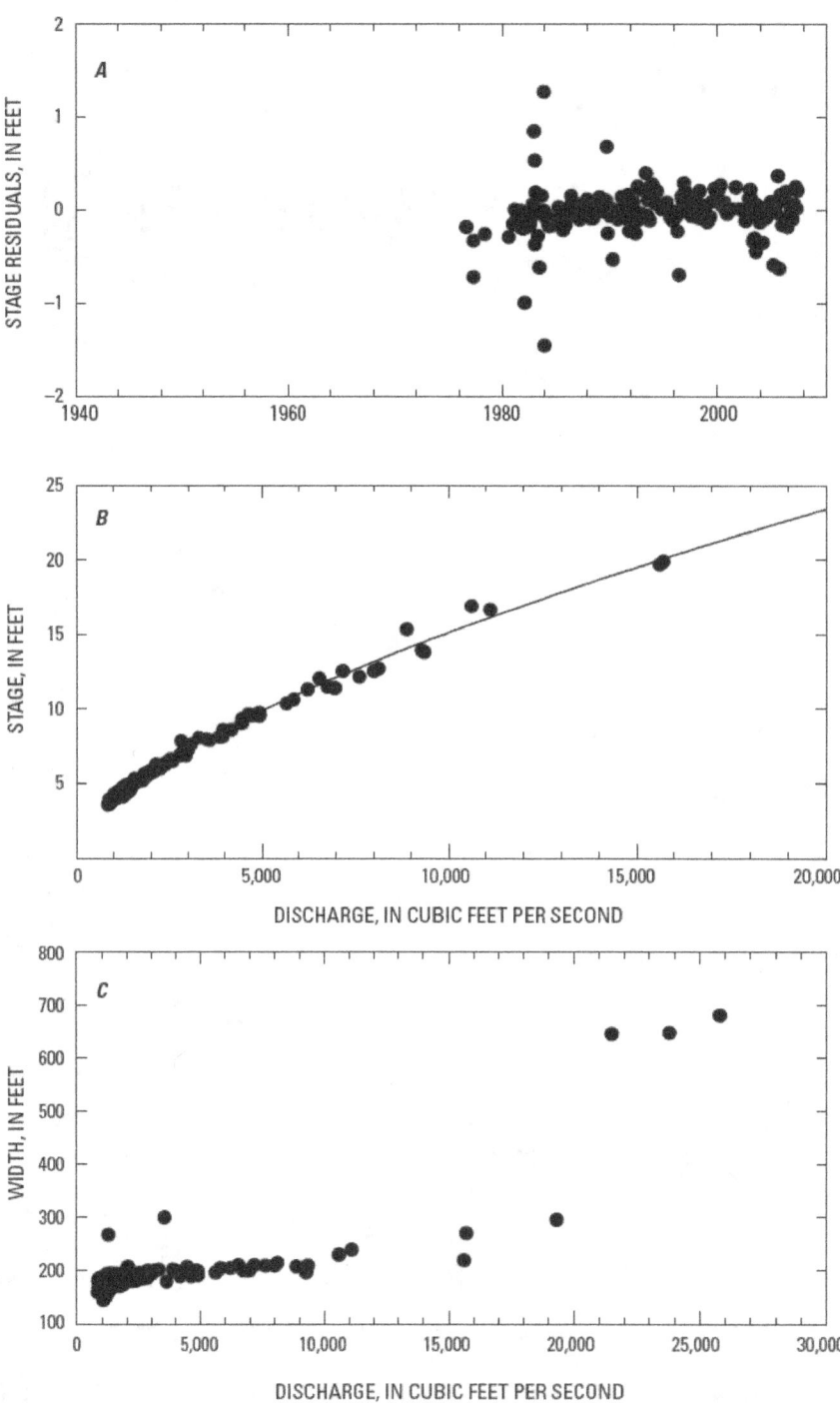

Figure 26.   Geomorphic analysis of streamgage data for Chattahoochee River at GA 280, near Atlanta, GA (station number 02336490): *(A)* time series of stage residuals; *(B)* stage and discharge; and *(C)* width and discharge.

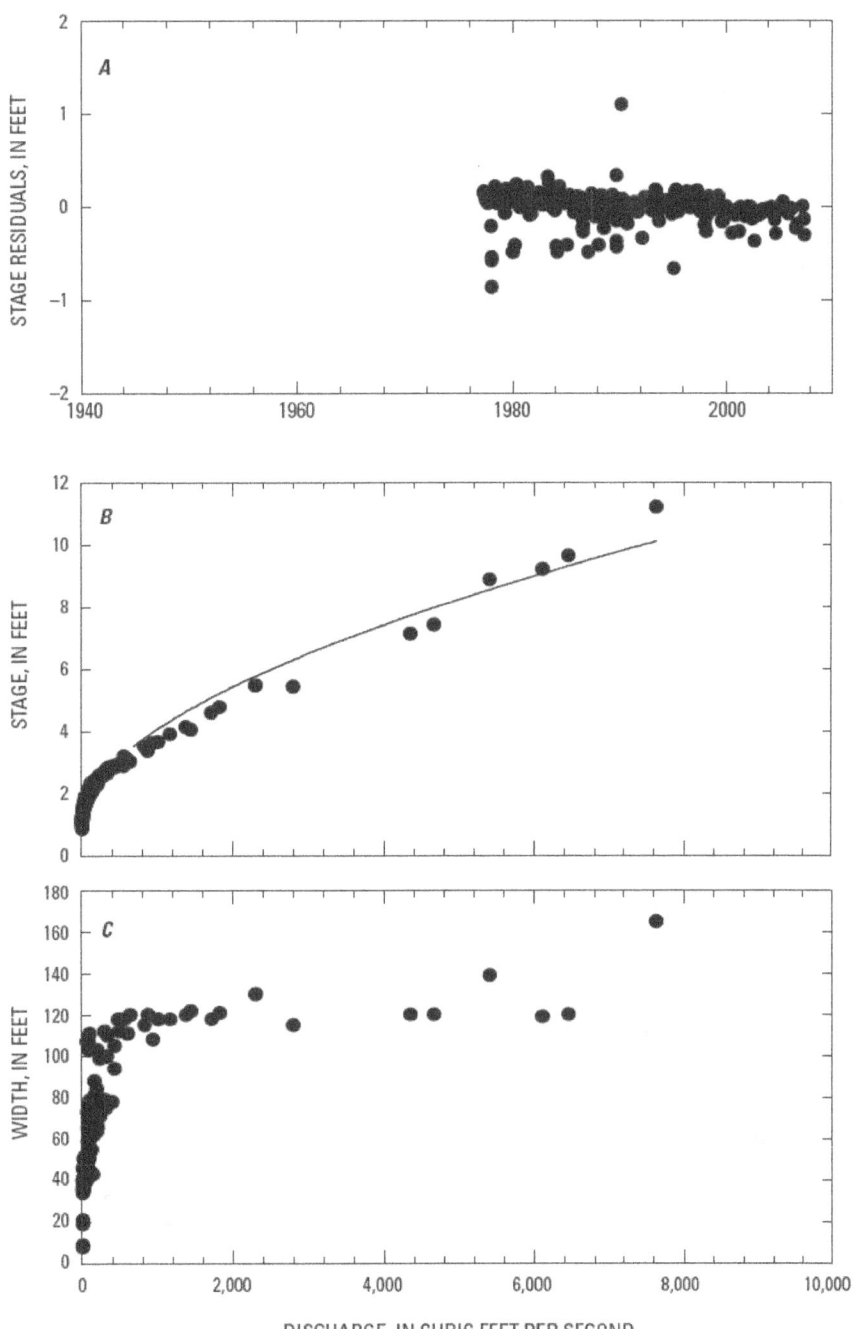

Figure 27. Geomorphic analysis of streamgage data for Murder Creek below Eatonton, GA (station number 02221525): *(A)* time series of stage residuals; *(B)* stage and discharge; and *(C)* width and discharge.

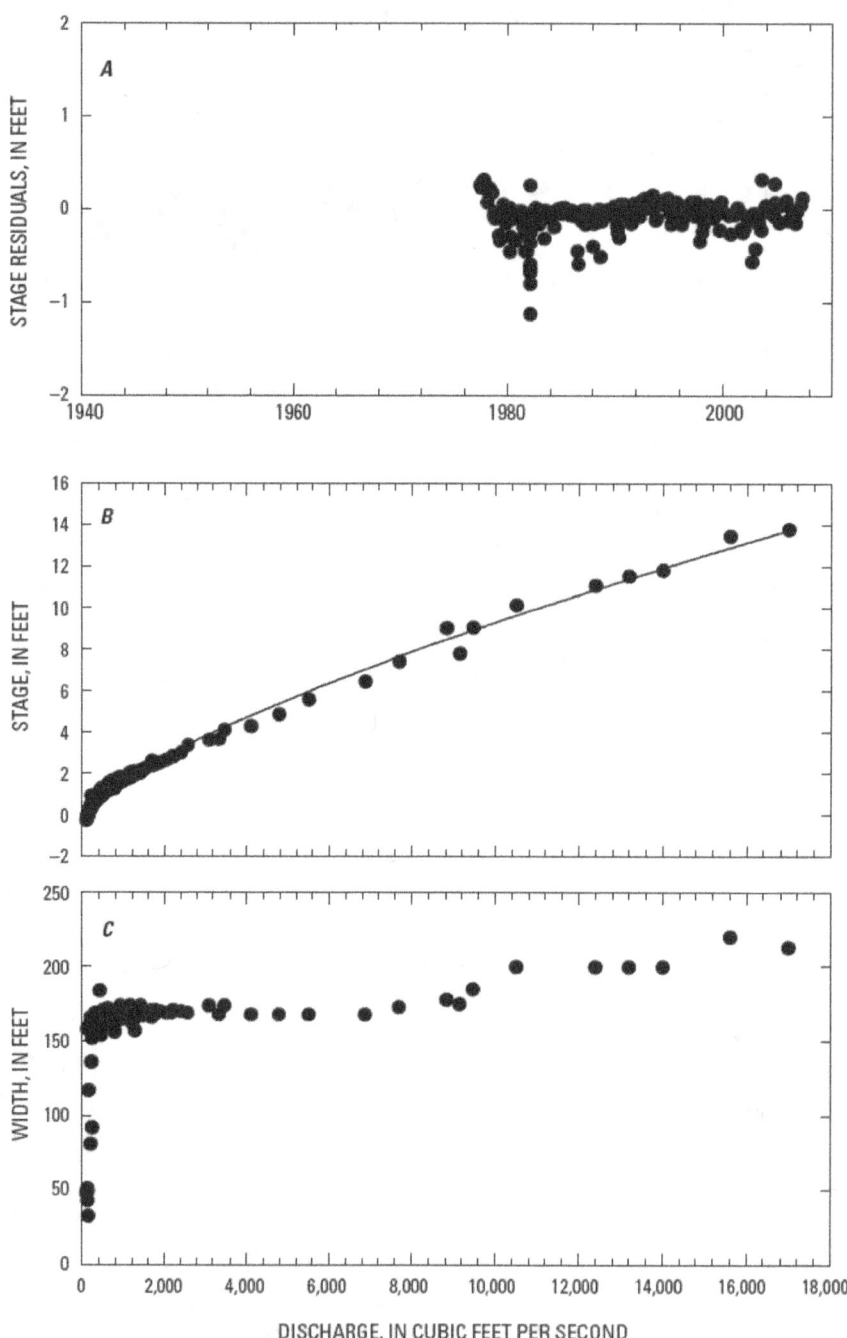

Figure 28.   Geomorphic analysis of streamgage data for Chattahoochee River near Cornellia, GA (station number 02331600): *(A)* time series of stage residuals; *(B)* stage and discharge; and *(C)* width and discharge.

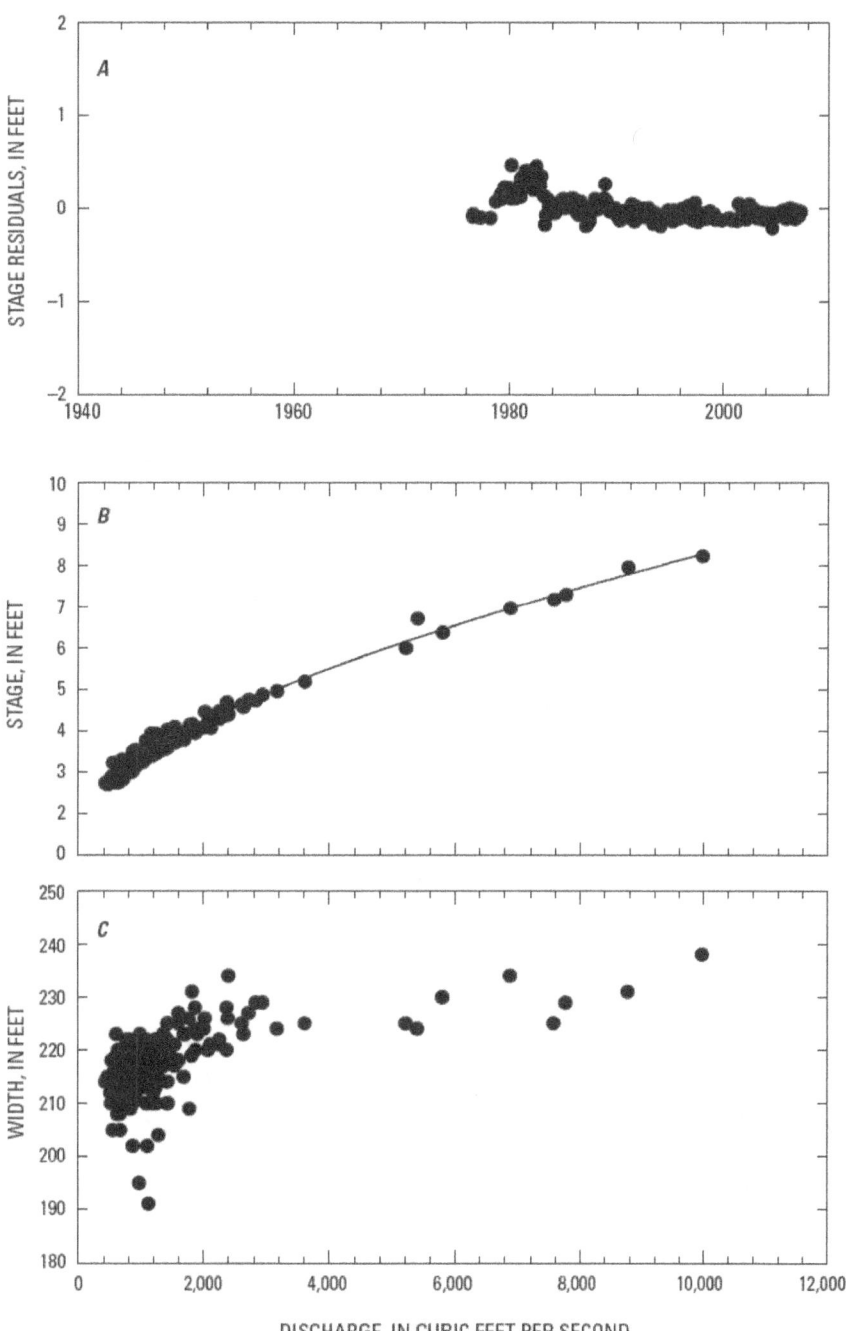

Figure 29. Geomorphic analysis of streamgage data for Chattahoochee River above Roswell, GA (station number 02335450): *(A)* time series of stage residuals; *(B)* stage and discharge; and (C) width and discharge.

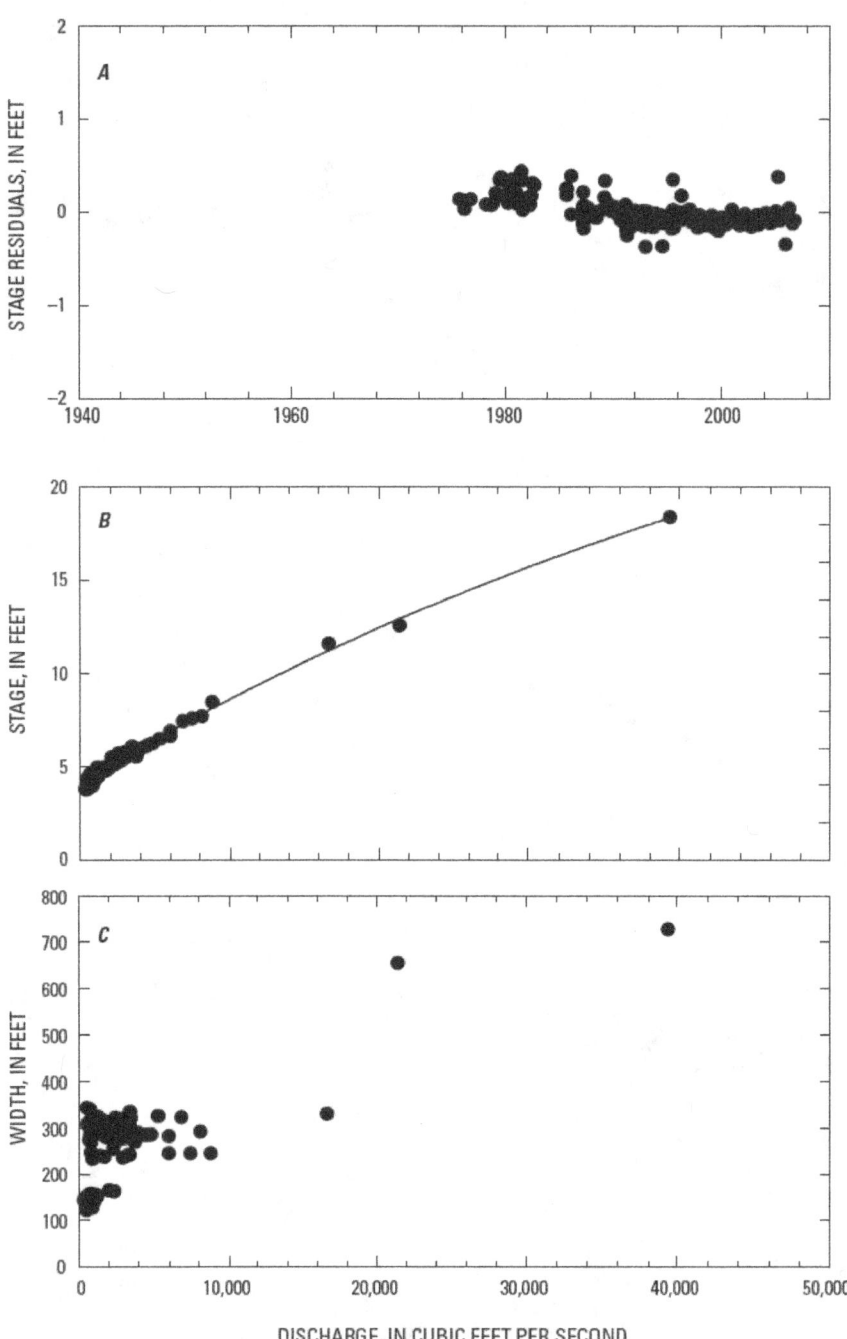

Figure 30.   Geomorphic analysis of streamgage data for Ocmulgee River near Jackson, GA (station number 02210500): *(A)* time series of stage residuals; *(B)* stage and discharge; and *(C)* width and discharge.

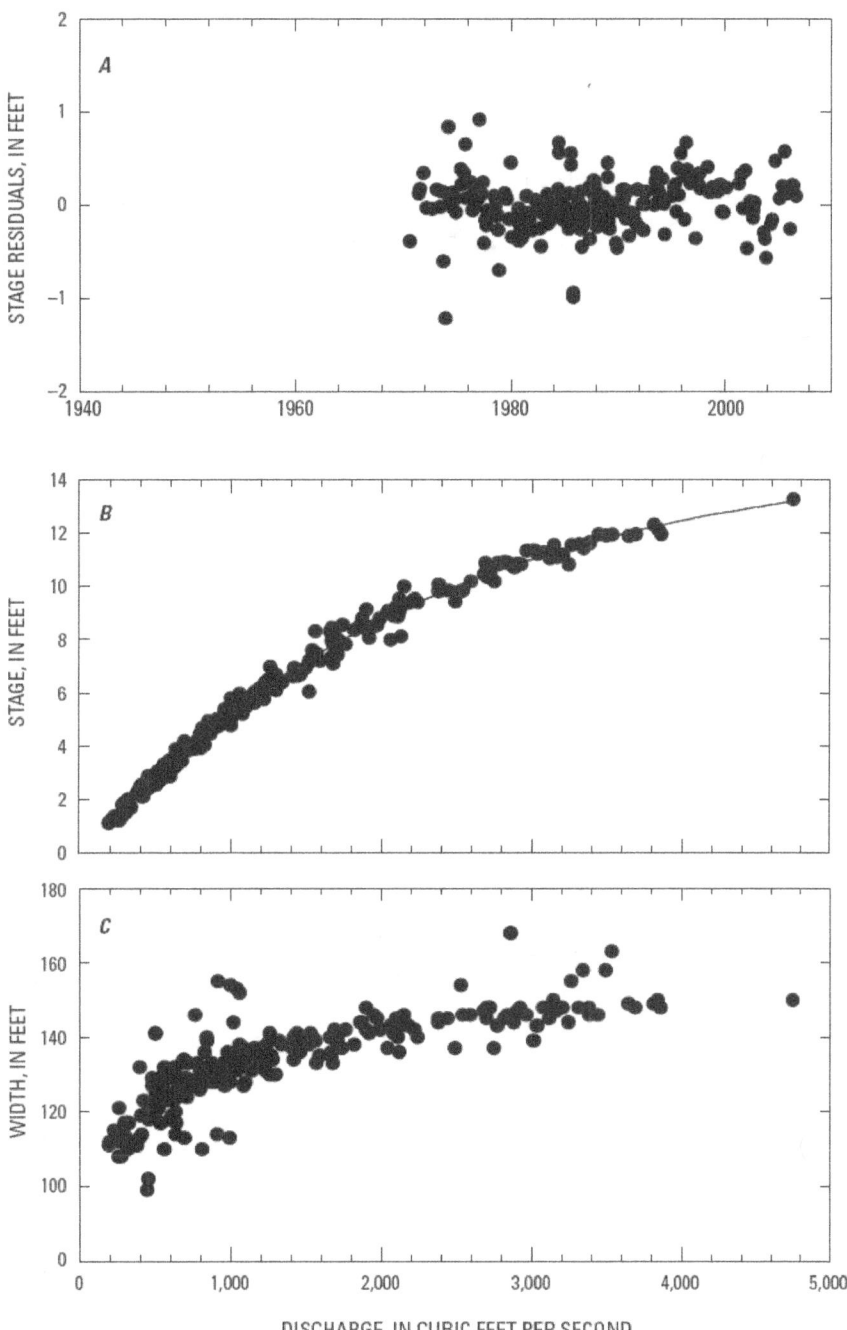

Figure 31. Geomorphic analysis of streamgage data for Ocmulgee River near Warner Robins, GA (station number 02213700): *(A)* time series of stage residuals; *(B)* stage and discharge; and *(C)* width and discharge.

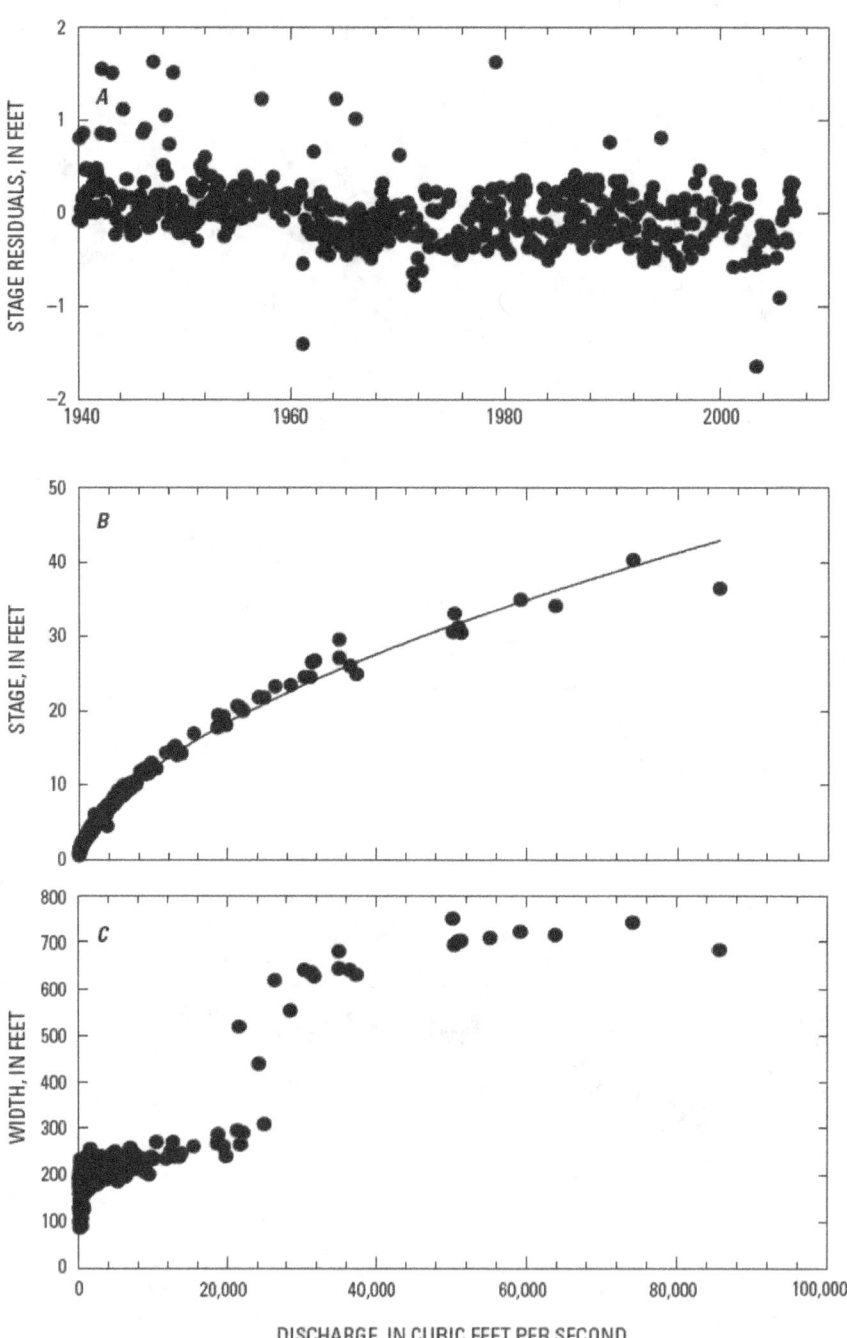

Figure 32. Geomorphic analysis of streamgage data for Flint River at U.S. 19, near Carsonville, GA (station number 02347500): *(A)* time series of stage residuals; *(B)* stage and discharge; and *(C)* width and discharge.

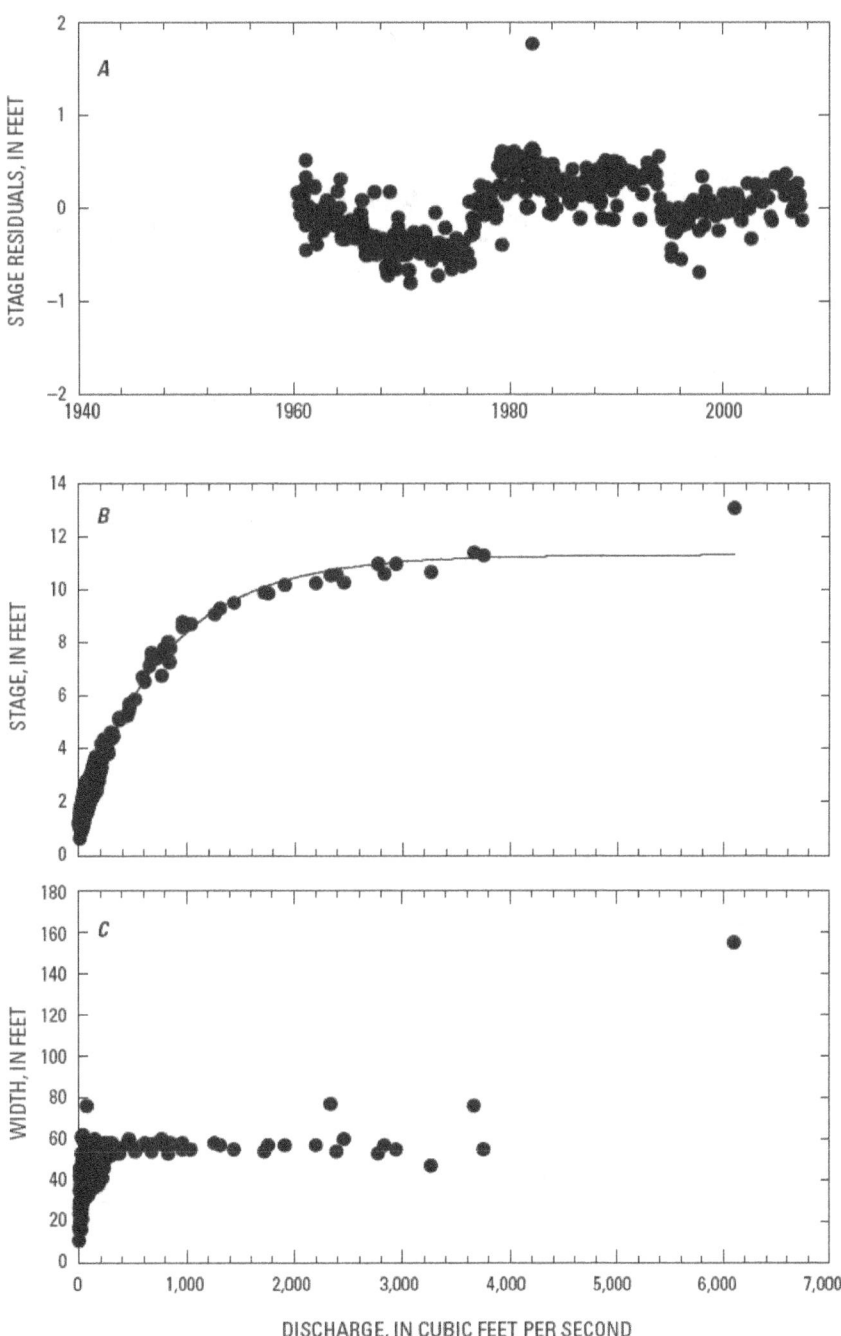

Figure 33. Geomorphic analysis of streamgage data for Big Creek near Alpharetta, GA (station number 02335700): *(A)* time series of stage residuals; *(B)* stage and discharge; and *(C)* width and discharge.

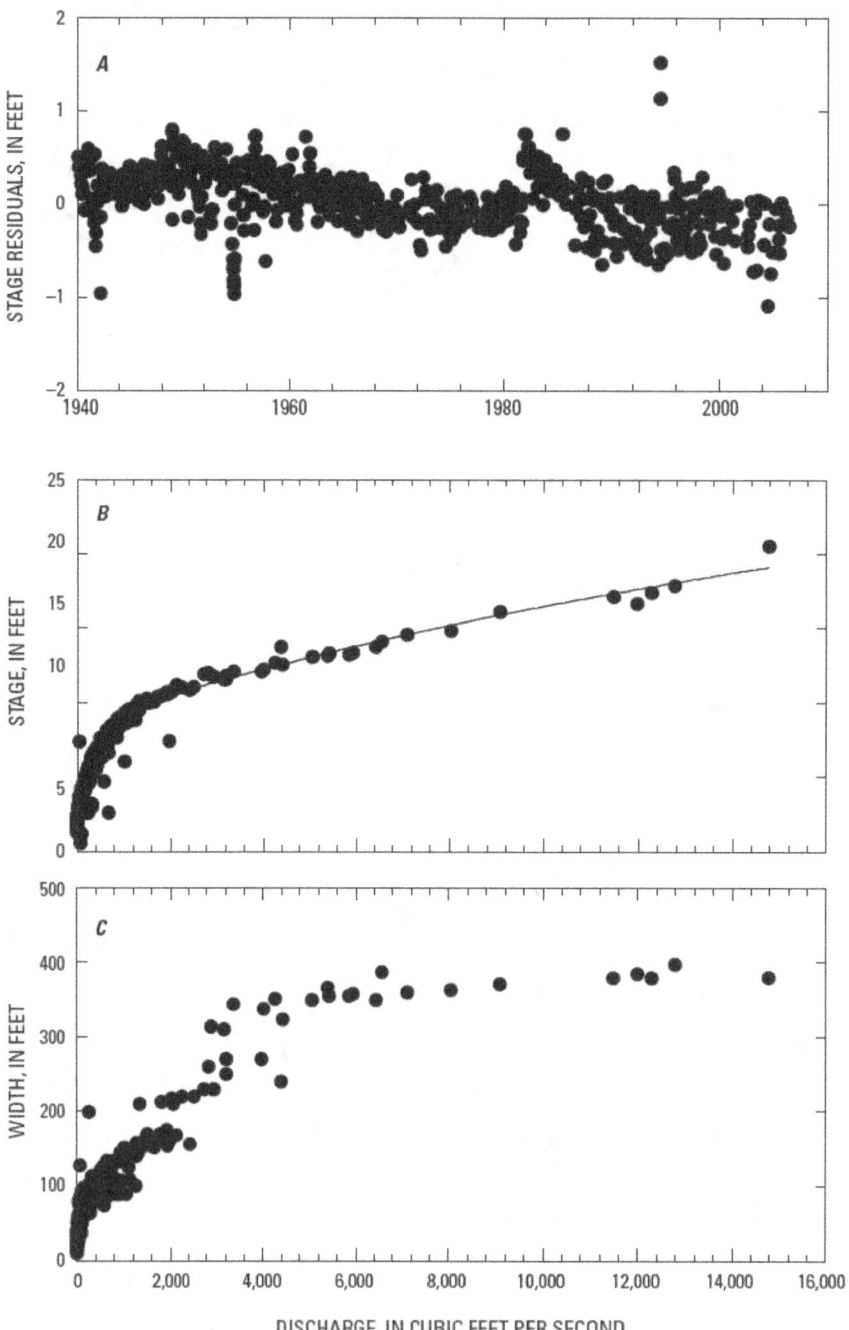

Figure 34.   Geomorphic analysis of streamgage data for Flint River near Griffin, GA (station number 02344500): *(A)* time series of stage residuals; *(B)* stage and discharge; and *(C)* width and discharge.

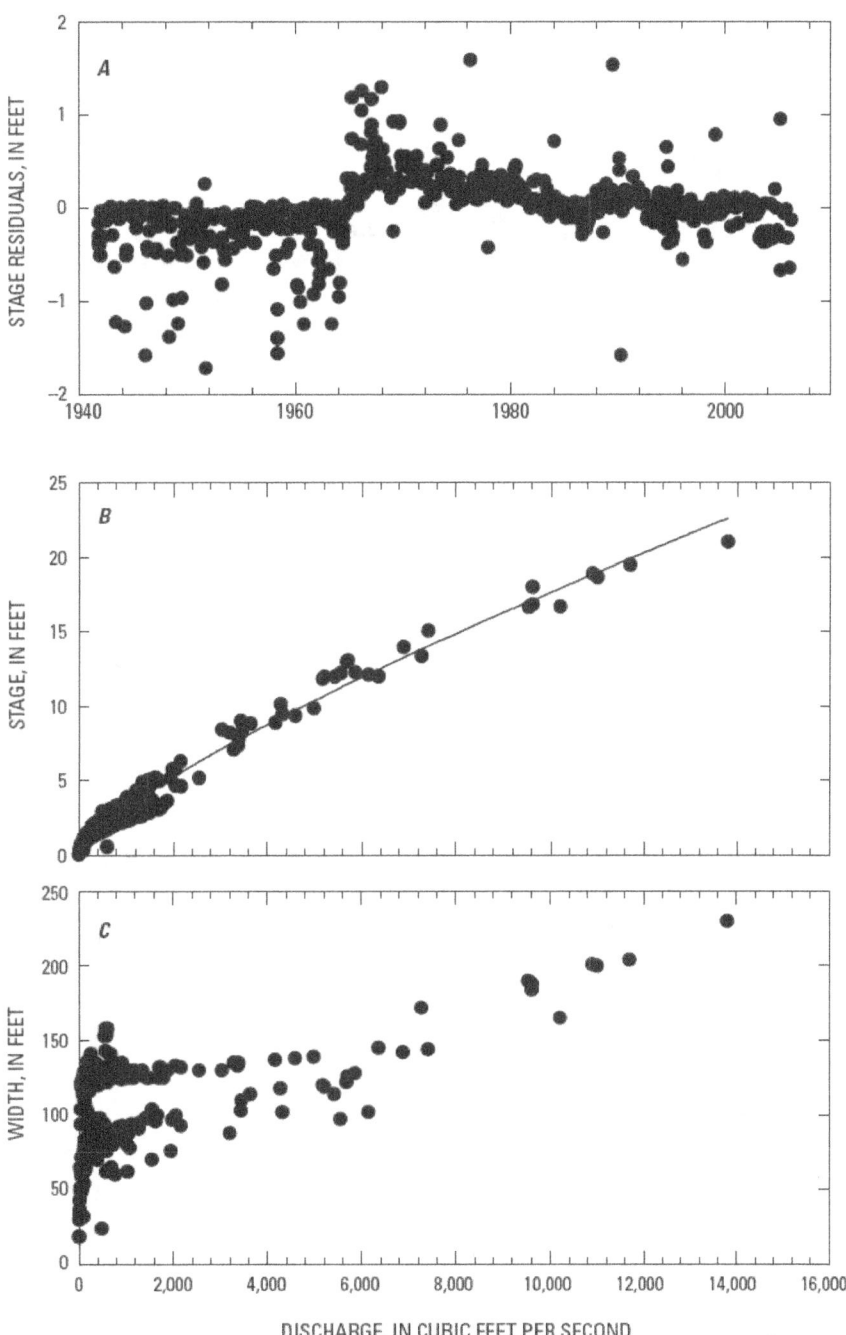

Figure 35.   Geomorphic analysis of streamgage data for Middle Oconee River near Athens, GA (station number 02217500): *(A)* time series of stage residuals; *(B)* stage and discharge; and *(C)* width and discharge.

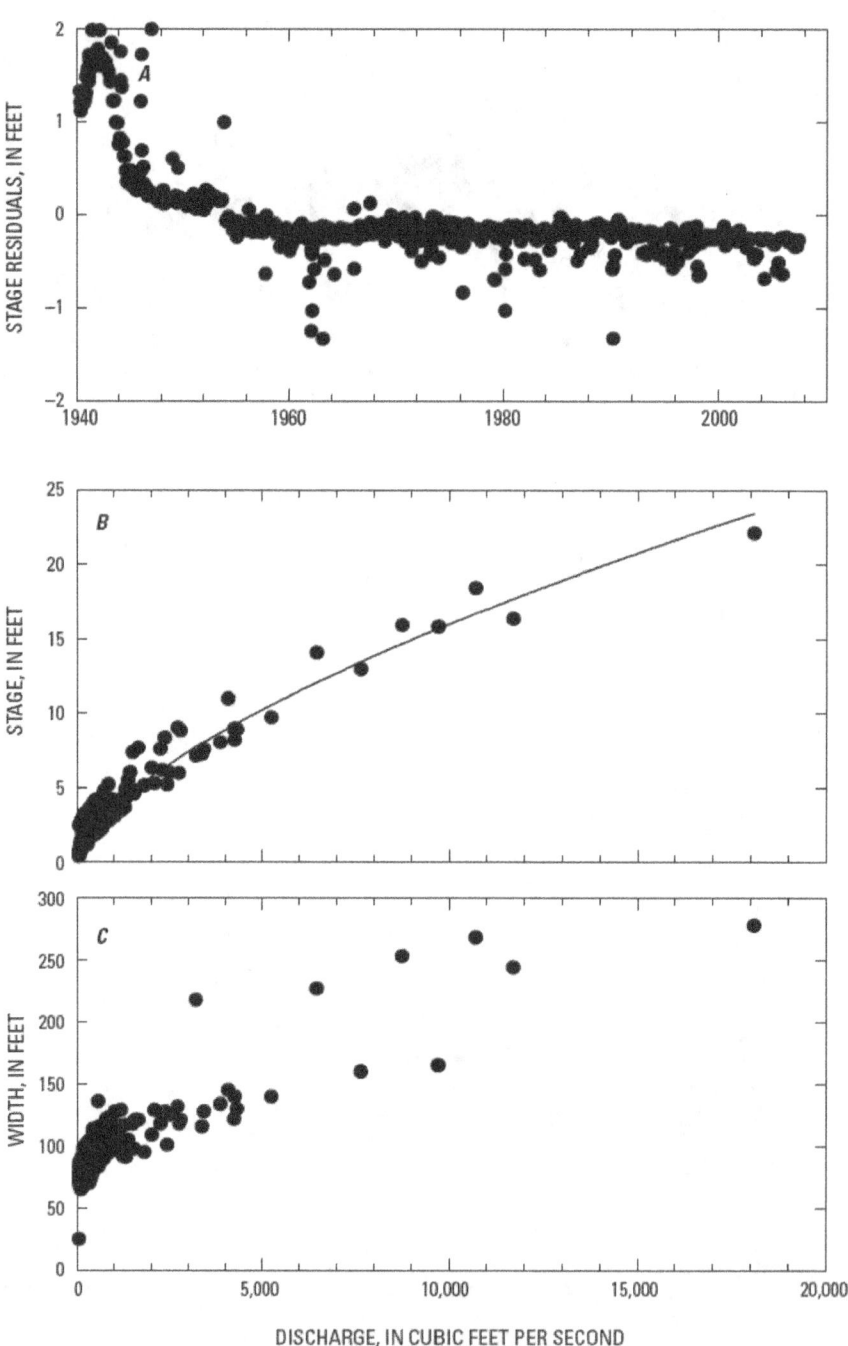

Figure 36.   Geomorphic analysis of streamgage data for Chestatee River near Dahlonega, GA (station number 02333500): *(A)* time series of stage residuals; *(B)* stage and discharge; and *(C)* width and discharge.

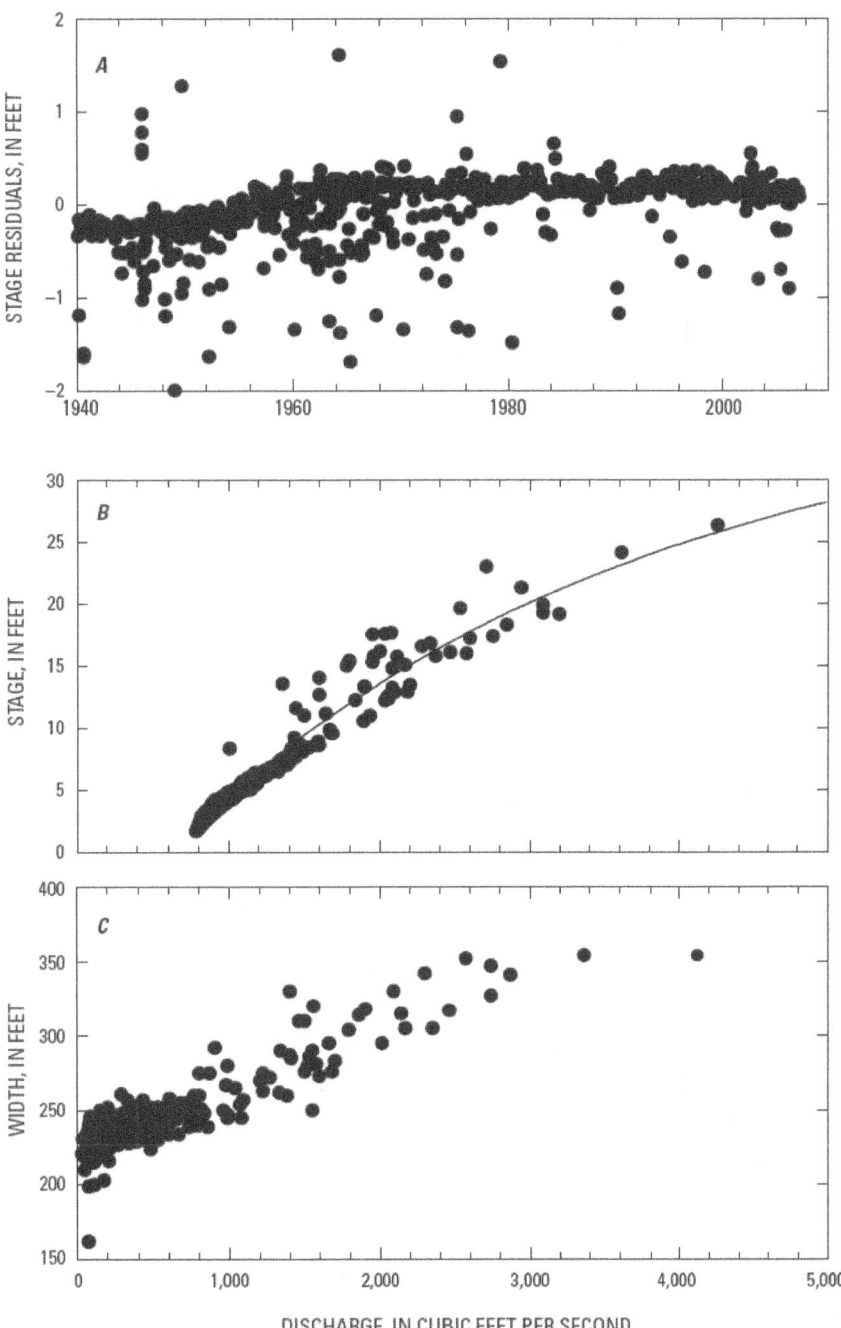

Figure 37. Geomorphic analysis of streamgage data for Chattahoochee River at Atlanta, GA (station number 02336000): *(A)* time series of stage residuals; *(B)* stage and discharge; and *(C)* width and discharge.

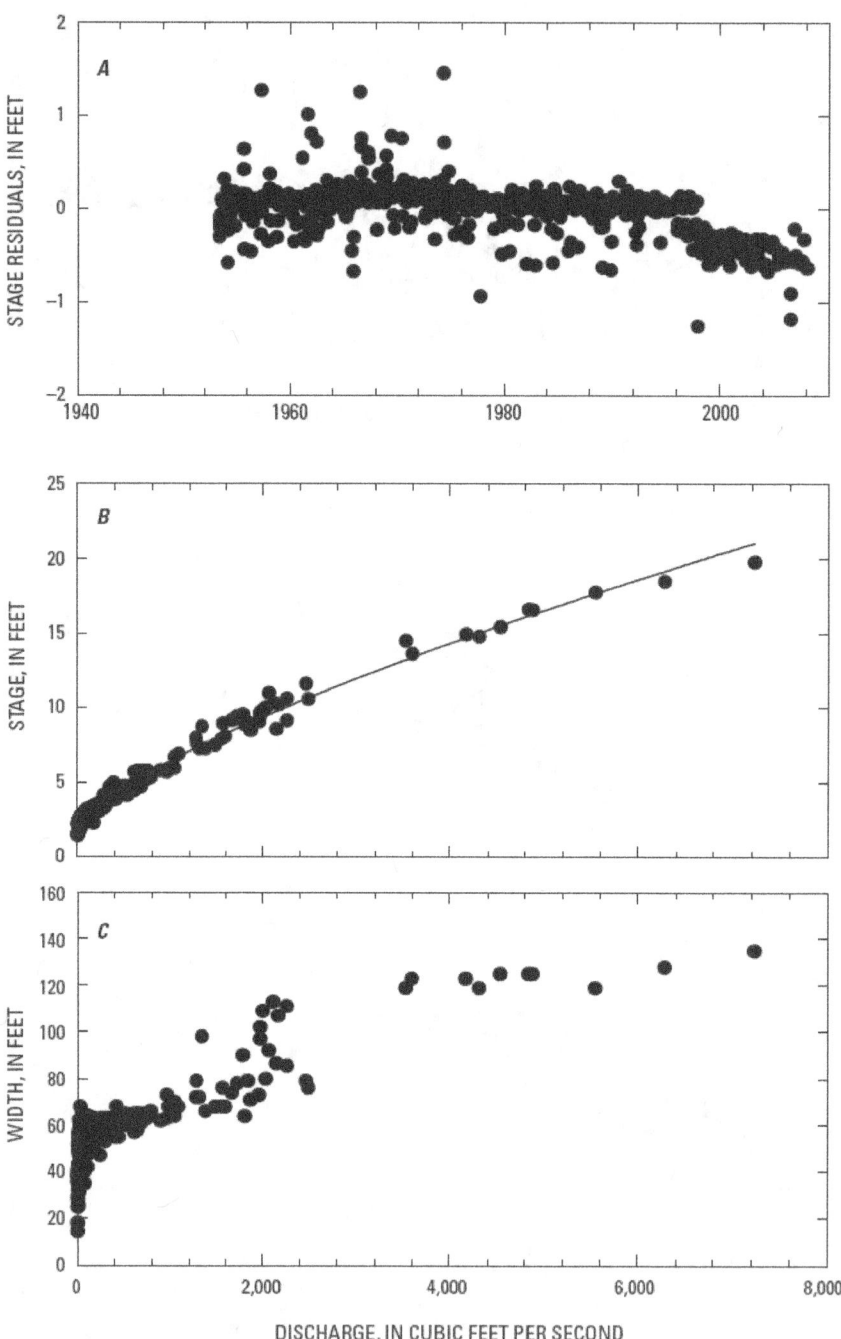

Figure 38.   Geomorphic analysis of streamgage data for Tobesofkee Creek near Macon, GA (station number02213500): *(A)* time series of stage residuals; *(B)* stage and discharge; and *(C)* width and discharge.

Manuscript approved on September 18, 2009
For more information about this publication contact:
    Jeffrey W. Riley
    USGS Georgia Water Science Center
    3039 Amwiler Road
    Atlanta, GA 30360
    Telephone: 770-903-9100
    E-mail: jriley@usgs.gov